SEE YOUR WAY
TO SELF-ESTEEM

*An In-Depth Study
Of the Causes & Cures
Of Low Self-Esteem*

Peter Michaelson

**Prospect
Books**

See Your Way To
SELF-ESTEEM

Peter Michaelson

Library of Congress Catalog Card Number: 92-62627

Publisher's Cataloging in Publication Data
Michaelson, Peter
See Your Way to Self-Esteem: An In-Depth Study of the Causes and
Cures of Low Self-Esteem.
Bibliography: p
1. Self-actualization (psychology). 2. Personal growth. 3. Applied
psychology. 4. Psychoanalysis.

ISBN 1-882631-25-0

Manufactured in the United States of America

Cover art by Peter Michaelson

First **Prospect Books** Edition July 1993
P.O. Box 8362, Santa Fe, NM. 87501

Acknowledgment

This book proves the adage that two minds are better than one. I suspect sometimes that Sandra, my wife and fellow psychotherapist, put as much insight into this book as I did. I marvel at her grasp of psychology and am so grateful to have her on my team.

Author's Note

The names and identifying details of the case histories in this book have been changed to protect confidentiality. Any resemblance to persons living or dead is purely coincidental. Anyone with a history of emotional disorders, or who feels emotionally unstable, or who is taking psychiatric medication, should not do the exercises in this book without first consulting a mental-health professional.

Table of Contents

PART II — Origins and Examples

PART III — Solutions and Remedies

Part I

Defining the Problem

The Search for Inner Value

The search for ways to instill and develop self-esteem has become the Holy Grail of educators, social reformers, and mental-health professionals. More than ever, self-esteem is regarded as the essential ingredient for enhancing success, happiness, and creativity, while reducing addictions, poverty, crime, and violence.

Raising the self-esteem of the population is, I believe, critical for boosting the nation's fortunes and bringing about political harmony, social justice, and prosperity.

Yet, even mental-health professionals find it hard to define self-esteem. For starters, it is an elusive inner quality that cannot be understood or treated independently of an individual's complete psychological makeup.

Before you can improve your self-esteem, you have to understand the roots of low self-esteem in the unconscious mind. This involves a process of assimilating a growing awareness of how your self-defeating beliefs and attitudes originate and how they are maintained.

A man came into my office and told me, "I know what my problem is—low self-esteem. So tell me how to fix it."

"Low self-esteem is a complicated problem," I said. "It is multi-faceted and no one answer will solve it. The problem cannot be separated from a person's whole psychology, his whole development. Raising self-esteem involves the unraveling of childhood perceptions, freeing blocked negative feelings, seeing your unconscious willingness to hold onto negative feelings, and dealing with problems of guilt, passivity, and aggression. You have to unlock secrets in your unconscious mind and discover the mystery of your own being."

The primary element in low self-esteem, I told him, is the feeling of being looked down upon by others as inadequate and unworthy. The problem is a consequence of a preoccupation with how you imagine others see you and how you see yourself.

If you have low self-esteem, you feel yourself to be inadequate, less than, ineffective, and flawed. Feeling worthless inside, you anticipate that others also see you as nothing special, less than, even worthless. People with low self-esteem spend a lot of time imagining that others see them as fakes and frauds.

A client revealed the essence of feelings of low self-esteem when he told me, "Whenever someone comes toward me with a smile, apparently happy to see me, I'm tempted to look back over my shoulder to make sure he's really looking at me."

Even intelligent, good-looking, prosperous people have problems to some degree with low self-esteem. The problem is definitely emotional and defies logical thinking. The solution involves bringing into our conscious minds the manner in which we are attached to negative and irrational impressions of ourselves and the methods whereby we maintain and re-inforce those negative impressions.

The following criteria reveal problems of low self-esteem:

i) an unwillingness to pursue goals and aspirations for fear of failure, even though you are capable or talented;

ii) an inability to take criticism and own up to your mistakes;

iii) obsessive thinking about your appearance and a frequent craving for the approval of others;

iv) an inability to be intimate for fear of being rejected or controlled;

v) an acceptance and toleration of abusive relationships;

vi) feelings of helplessness and powerlessness in getting ahead in your career aspirations;

vii) an attitude of defeat and hopelessness about your life;

viii) a feeling that what success you do have is not good enough or that others will ridicule your accomplishments;

ix) difficulty having fun; and an inability to receive good in your life.

Self-esteem is the feeling of appreciating your own inner value as a human being, independently of your accomplishments or standing in the world. Many people who are rich and famous are still unable to appreciate fully their own inner value. But a slave may be able to feel it, even as he sees others looking at him as if he were nothing. Self-esteem is a feeling of being at peace with yourself, and this quality may have little bearing on external circumstances.

To have self-esteem means to respect yourself, to stand up for yourself, to honor yourself, and *at the same time* to be compassionate and sensitive to others. Self-esteem is the ability to believe in yourself and to bring out the best in yourself, while according others that same respect and acknowledgement.

At the heart of low self-esteem is the fear of being yourself. This fear causes an individual to suppress his feelings and creative abilities. It stops him from being expressive, involved, and spontaneous.

What would happen if, when you are around others, you let yourself be just who you are? Most people will say, "They will laugh at me." Or, "They will be disgusted, see me as a fake, see me as weak and worthless, think I'm stupid, reject me, scorn me, put me down, ignore me, or dismiss me."

As a consequence of this fear of being and expressing ourselves, we live in fear in our relationships with others, and abort opportunities to enhance our creative accomplishments. We are apt to choose inappropriate partners in relationships, ignore our health, inwardly feel rejected and unloved, and find ourselves in frequent conflict with others.

We are quick to feel guilt, worry, anxiety, boredom, loneliness, jealousy, depression, apathy, and to be preoccupied with how we are seen by others. Often we become addicts, compulsives, and phobics—but mostly we are everyday people who can't quite get our lives shifted into high gear.

Fear of being yourself indicates an expectation of being denied, controlled, rejected or condemned in some way. Current realities are not responsible for these feelings so much as experiences and perceptions retained from our childhood. As children, most of us experienced that we were frequently doing something wrong and that our parents did not approve of our self-expression.

In absorbing this feeling, we developed a harsh inner conscience. As adults, we continue to be plagued with the same guilt, shame, and inner reproach we experienced in our family of origin. The inner conscience, which replaces the harshness we felt from our parents, is always ready to attack us for the slightest misdeeds or alleged shortcomings. Feeling better about ourselves requires pacification of those critical inner voices, allowing us to be at peace with ourselves.

People may know *intellectually* that they are good and that being themselves will be acceptable and perhaps even attractive to others. But reasoning has little influence on the emotional course of our lives. People with low self-esteem are unable to experience being themselves for *emotional* reasons.

The problem with low self-esteem stems from *faulty perceptions*. The facts of a situation are discolored by our emotions. Unconsciously, we choose to see ourselves in a negative light, and we expect and imagine that others also see us in this light.

This book shows you how to neutralize those entrenched negative beliefs and feelings. The book has three parts: (i) defining the problem, (ii) origins and examples, and (iii) solutions and remedies. I want to emphasize that *understanding the depth and breadth of the problem is part of the solution*. We all would like a quick fix or an instant cure for our bad feelings about ourselves. Some readers may want to go straight to Part III for the solutions and remedies. However, the quality of your new house of self-esteem needs to rest on a solid foundation of knowledge and insight.

For those of you who want a better life, this book can transform how you perceive yourself and others. I can give you the blueprint, the tools, and even the building materials— but you are the one to raise up your new house.

The knowledge in this book will challenge many people, especially those who want to make others responsible for their bad feelings and failures. People with low self-esteem resist acknowledgment of how they cooperate unconsciously in every negative emotion or experience. But only when you take responsibility for yourself, will you be free to make positive changes in your life.

Unlike other self-help books that focus on superficial solutions, this book peeps into the mysteries of the unconscious mind. You will see that your unconscious mind is a primary source of understanding and insight, and the seat of great power and influence.

Time for a Change

How do you change? How do you go from chronic misery to everyday zest for life? Is it even possible?

Consciously, everyone wants to be happy. But we are all up against a sabotaging side of ourselves that isn't at all interested in our happiness. Many people are ensnared emotionally by this negative side, and consequently they passively endure unhappiness and emotional hardships, believing that chronic emotional pain such as theirs is an unavoidable experience of life.

That's not the way it has to be, providing you can acquire insight, the most powerful force for change. Insight requires that you see into yourself, understanding the faulty interpretations that are operating in your unconscious mind.

But people are not seeing beneath the surface into their unconscious or subconscious operations where negative beliefs and feelings are rooted. Even most mental-health professionals focus on surface symptoms, offering only behavioral advice and powder-puff techniques instead of insight into the origins of our emotional problems.

Most writings on self-esteem give readers various recommendations for boosting self-esteem: accept yourself, trust yourself and others, take risks, forgive yourself and others, express feelings, and take responsibility for your own decisions and actions. There's nothing wrong with those recommendations. But how are they manifested? How do you learn, for instance, to trust and accept yourself? Knowing that you need to trust and accept yourself is a long way from actually being able to trust and accept yourself.

The process requires extensive inventory of your unconscious feelings, beliefs, and motivations. You need to correlate these with your past experiences from childhood to see how you recreate in the present what is unresolved from the past. The process works like an *awakening,* opening your mind and feelings to a new sense of yourself.

So raising self-esteem involves a process of self-discovery. You discover your negative beliefs and feelings, and see how rooted they are in your psyche, how attached you are to them. Once you have unblocked what was keeping you from good feelings about yourself, trust and self-acceptance come to you automatically.

Every person has two aspects to his being—an intellectual side and an emotional side. Your intellectual side may know that you are a decent person, that you are loved by your family, and that people for the most part like you. But emotionally you keep getting tangled up in feeling inadequate, not good enough, somehow defective, maybe even worthless. So even when you know intellectually you are good and worthy, you may not be convinced emotionally.

That is because you carry within you a warehouse of emotional content that represents all the repressed feelings and memories from childhood of the ways in which you felt helpless, inadequate, and unworthy. The trick is to see and understand how those negative feelings are getting the better of you in your present life.

Rhonda, a client of mine, couldn't see what was blocking her from being herself. She knew she was passive and obliging, a real people-pleaser, and she hated herself for being weak and submissive. When others stated their opinions, Rhonda tended to see things their way. Most of the time she didn't even know her own mind.

"I doubt the value of my beliefs or feelings," she told me. "It doesn't occur to me to state my views. I'm not even sure I know what I'm thinking or feeling. I feel that others don't want to know what I have to say."

Rhonda didn't know how to be herself. She didn't trust her own judgment. She expected others to see her as weak and felt that they were out to invalidate her at every opportunity. Rhonda took any disagreement or sarcastic comments from others as rejection or devaluation of herself. It felt to her that others were out to hurt her deliberately and to put her down.

A mental-health professional suggested that Rhonda needed to become more assertive and not let people walk all over her. She took the advice. But now she went to the other extreme and became touchy, grouchy, and pushy. She blasted her friends with negative reactions to their behaviors and proposals. Her friends let her know that the new Rhonda was not much of an improvement. Instead of the old passivity and apathy, Rhonda was now tangled up in feelings of resentment and anger toward others.

She had not solved the basic problem—her tendency to feel controlled and looked down upon by others. Only when she understood the nature of this passivity was she able to avoid defensive reactions and assert herself appropriately.

"Your unhappiness is a mystery to be solved," I told her. "You have to begin to see and understand how negative and positive elements clash like titans in the inner sanctum of your mind. You fall into the negative or generate negativity, whenever you *feel or imagine,* regardless of the actual circumstances, that someone is controlling you, telling you what to do or disapproving of you. You interpret control and disapproval even when no one is attempting to control you or disapprove of you at all."

Rhonda's tendency to become entangled in feelings of being forced to submit to the will of others started in her childhood. Her father had been strict and authoritarian, and she had cultivated the emotional conviction that he knew what was best for her and what was expected of her. She believed it was bad even to question his iron rule. Her father's domination left her feeling insecure and fearful. But she didn't know any other way to experience her life with him.

Rhonda convinced herself emotionally that she was the problem and not her father. She felt inadequate, less than, and unworthy, and she began to act out what she believed was the reality. Her whole being took on this self-image in her tone of voice, body language, demeanor, and behavior. Becoming inadequate was the only way to claim control over her father's domination and ward off her extreme feelings of helplessness.

"A part of you," I continued, "is very tempted to slip into negative feelings through doorways marked 'control issues' and 'disapproval issues.' And you will play one of two roles: the helpless person feeling disapproved of or controlled or the one who wants to control and disapprove of others. Either way you lose. The more you see how you set yourself up to be controlled and indulge in feeling disapproved of, the more you will lose interest in these self-defeating games.

"Rhonda, you have been afraid to be yourself. You believe emotionally that others will disapprove of you if you do not behave the way you believe they expect you to. So you don't consider yourself. You have a hard time valuing or honoring yourself because you look to others, not yourself, for direction and for a sense of who you are. If others disapprove of you, you immediately feel that disapproval is valid. If others appear to want to control you, you immediately feel threatened, as if they could actually take possession of you and force you to submit to their will.

"You become preoccupied with yourself because all you see is how you imagine others see and feel about you. In your imagination, everything revolves around you, and you put yourself at the mercy, emotionally speaking, of what others may or may not be thinking and saying about you.

"This can all be remedied, Rhonda. We are going to help you change the way you see yourself and others."

And she did change. "I'm just amazed, just amazed," Rhonda said months later. "My suffering was all a result of what I didn't see and understand about myself. I can't get over the irony: I thought I knew myself and I knew almost nothing."

Some people are not aware they have a problem of low self-esteem. The problem often crashes down on middle-aged professionals or business people who suddenly find themselves in an emotional crisis. One example is the workaholic whose frantic pace is based not on love of work but on the emotional conviction that he is nothing without it. He makes this discovery of his inner deficiency when he is suddenly unemployed without a sense of inner strength to sustain him. Another example is the woman who remains subservient to the needs and aspirations of her successful husband, and who suddenly finds herself divorced or widowed without any career skills or self-confidence.

Low self-esteem is also realized when people react with panic at the prospect of financial loss, when they falter inexplicably in their career aspirations, when they realize they have taken on too much responsibility for others, when they recognize their compulsive need for approval, or when they see that their relationships have been superficial or phony.

Unfortunately, they often run to a medical doctor for anti-depressants or tranquilizers rather than explore and over-come the root causes of their emotional difficulties.

Levels of Self-Esteem

Our progress toward feeling good about ourselves can be seen and experienced through what I call the five levels of self-esteem: *thinking, feeling, seeing, willing,* and *being.*

Let's start with *thinking,* the basic level. All humans think, and some think more clearly and precisely than others. The primary problem at this level, other than muddled and confused thinking, is the tendency of many people to experience their minds and their thoughts as being at the center of their existence.

A lot of people think that logic and reason have the answers for most everything. But they are only comforting themselves emotionally with the conviction that their minds are in charge of every situation.

We are trained in school to honor and revere the rational mind. But rationality is only an aspect of ourselve—an ability or a gift. However, people become so mesmerized by the mental side of their nature that they begin to believe that the mental side is the only point of view they have.

The mental side is an important tool to interact with our

world. But it is not the only way to understand reality. If the mental aspect is used exclusively for your guidance and direction, you'll lead yourself down a blind alley.

Then your self becomes subservient to your mind, and you are held spellbound by what your mind is producing in the way of thoughts, memories, speculations, or facts. In your sense of identity, it's as if your thoughts represent who and what you are. You are much more, of course. But if you don't experience yourself more expansively, your sense of self is greatly impoverished. Our logical, rational mind focuses on thoughts, facts, memories, speculations, and data collecting. It emphasizes dealing with ourselves from a logical mode rather than a feeling or intuitive mode. The focus on the mental wants to explain or analyze things rather than feel what's going on.

For instance, because doctors can't explain how acupuncture works, some of them believe the procedure has no value. They have no mode to evaluate it other than the rational. But for many people who try acupuncture, how it works is incidental to the benefits. A lot of things in nature work independently of our ability to fathom them.

That your mind is at the center of your being is an illusion, a dangerous one. There are drives and energies shaping your mental processes, including subconscious forces that are impersonal, even alien, and operate independently of any consideration for your well-being.

Let's move on to the second level, *feelings*. A major element in self-esteem is the ability to express what you are feeling in your own heart, in your own soul. Then you are honoring yourself, expressing yourself, speaking up for yourself, remembering yourself, and knowing who you are.

A great deal of awareness about reality comes through our feelings, and people who are developing their capacity for happiness begin to feel their way into a new sense of themselves as they integrate and assimilate the hurt, memories, and feelings from their past.

It may be easy for us to talk about what we are *thinking* and much harder to talk about what we are *feeling*. One reason is that as children we often felt that our feelings were discounted and seen as irrelevant. We were not encouraged to express our feelings. Often parents were quick to explain away our feelings, to rationalize our feelings. Usually they wanted to take away the pain of bad feelings by explaining them away.

But often it isn't bad feelings a child is expressing so much as the range of feelings that explore his or her own being. A feeling is just a feeling. Even if it is irrational, such as fear of the dark, the feeling needs to be acknowledged because it is the child's experience. If parents discount the child's experience such as sadness or fear or anger, it feels to the child that his or her own self is being discounted. Then the child won't trust his feelings, and he won't trust himself.

Sometimes people don't know the difference between thinking and feeling. I have asked clients how they *feel* about something, and heard them reply, "I *think* that . . ." If you are at a party, you might think, "People are jerks, this party is boring." At the same time, you might *feel* (without even articulating it), "I am out of place here, I don't belong, people don't find me interesting."

As another example, I asked a man how he *felt* about his wife's criticism of him, and he told me why he *thought* she was wrong in her comments to him. He didn't tell me how her criticism made him *feel* because he interpreted the experience mentally rather than feeling it. On some level, however, he did indeed feel the effect of her criticism, but he wasn't "plugged in" to this part of himself. He was so mental that he didn't monitor himself on a feeling level. He was only aware of a generalized resentment toward her that was expressed in his passive-aggressive defiance and withholding.

Self-esteem itself is a feeling. It's the ability to be yourself based on a feeling of confidence that you have about yourself. So if your expression of feelings is blocked, you are limited in how good you can feel about yourself.

Self-esteem means trusting your feelings. It means valuing your feelings. Your feelings don't even have to be right. For instance, when you express feelings of hurt, those feelings don't have to be right or to be justified by circumstances. Someone else in your shoes might not feel hurt in the same situation—but that does not mean that your experience is wrong. Your feelings are an expression of you. Not to be able to express them means not to value yourself.

It is true that certain feelings such as anger or defiance can be defenses covering up some passivity in you. So you have to understand why you are feeling angry, lonely, defiant, or whatever and define the underlying hurt that is prompting that feeling.

And that brings us to level three, *seeing*. This book is titled, *See Your Way To Self-Esteem*, and is all about the need for self-awareness or insight to improve how we feel about ourselves. Now, some people can have strong self-esteem without seeing a whole lot into their psychology. They are naturals in the art of self-respect. But for those with low self-esteem, seeing is a crucial step that makes it possible to transform themselves. It is the discovery of choices and the awareness that you have more options in how to respond to given situations, where previously you would have responded automatically in self-defeating ways.

Seeing also develops when the visual drive or emotional imagination (which I define beginning in the next chapter) comes under more conscious direction and control to align with your best interests.

Imagine that you are a detective and have taken on an assignment to uncover the mystery of your own low self-esteem. As you progress with this assignment, you see more and more into the mystery of what is involved in your low self-esteem. Over time, as you examine and study the relevant information, you see the mystery unfold as a series of insights which give you the clear, final picture.

The primary thing to see is your own involvement in your emotional difficulties, and that means seeing how you maintain, reinforce, and promote your own suffering. You see your unconscious tendencies to become entangled in negative feelings that are unresolved from your past, and you become aware of how you are compelled to act out these unresolved feelings with people in your present life.

You see that your current emotional difficulties are related to past experiences and that you are unconsciously willing to perpetuate childhood feelings of deprivation, refusal, rejection, criticism, and passive submission to the control of others.

I told one client whose self-esteem was affected by her tendencies to cultivate feelings of abandonment, criticism, and deprival: "When you get into those feelings, you are moving into a negative experience of yourself and of life. You want to begin to see your own role in this, how a part of you will take different situations to indulge in feelings of being abandoned, or criticized, or deprived. You see how you are limiting your chances for success and happiness—no matter how smart or determined you are—because of these unconscious impulses, patterns, and tendencies.

"Once you see this process, you will also see that you have choices in how to respond to situations. If you don't see what's involved here, you will be easily caught in negative experiences, as well as the prospect of self-defeating behavior, with no insight to help you to untangle yourself."

Next in the progression of self-esteem is *willing*. Don't confuse willing with will-power. Self-defeating people can still muster up a lot of will-power in specific circumstances. A greedy man with $10 million in the bank can use will-power to go out in the world and cheat others out of another $10 million.

Will-power can be driven by self-interest, while willing is a higher manifestation of our humanity that is driven by the wish to excel, to master, and to defeat that which is negative.

Willing is a feeling, a kind of inner energy or a refined emotional resolve, that is aligned with your well-being. It is the ability to put into action that which you know is wise and in your best interest and to follow up on new choices you see available to you. It comes into its own behind the power of clear thinking, liberated feelings, and deep insight. Willing is not so much a fight against something as it is a harmony with what is and what can be.

It is a feeling of valuing yourself to such a degree that you are unwilling to settle for less. You are determined to bring out the best in yourself, for your sake and for others.

Finally, there is *being.* This defines your ability to appreciate yourself for *who you are* rather than for *what you do* or how you perform. At this level of experiencing yourself, you are able to respond to life's challenges and problems with an attitude of learning and a desire to understand, rather than with self-pity or defeatism.

You manifest new and more effective ways to develop rapport and intimacy with others. You feel at home in the world. Now you have the ability to generate love from within you and express it to those around you. You attract caring, loving people into your life who treat you with respect.

You define clearly what you want and where you want to go in your life and enjoy a feeling of gratitude for what you have as well as trust in a positive future. Life becomes stimulating and fun, and work becomes more creative and productive.

In a state of *being,* feelings of anger, irritation, and frustration have decreased greatly. The tendency to react defensively to perceived criticism is gone. You assert your rights and feelings appropriately without causing alienation from others. The tendency to judge others or to be preoccupied with their weaknesses has also waned.

The issues that produced misery and suffering in your life wither away and die. They are replaced by the development of your creative capacities and the ability to live by your own inner voice.

The Visual Connection

The hallmark of low self-esteem is feeling yourself to be inadequate, a failure, unsatisfactory in some manner, or not loveable. As you regard yourself as inadequate, you imagine that this is how you are seen by others.

Anticipating disapproval, rejection or condemnation from others makes it more likely for you to behave or act out in self-defeating ways that do indeed provoke others to look upon you as inadequate, a failure, and so on.

This process of imaging that others see us as deficient is an aspect of a mysterious function called the visual drive, or what I prefer to call *the emotional imagination*. The term refers to the tendency to imagine, see, and interpret events, situations, and other people according to our own subjective emotional perceptions. In other words, reality is an interpretation that we make. We learn what to perceive and, emotionally, we are what we perceive.

An important aspect of overcoming low self-esteem involves the discovery of how you have been misusing the visual drive or emotional imagination to keep alive negative perceptions of yourself and how others see you. This book uncovers the mysteries of the emotional imagination and reveals its intimate role in (i) unconsciously maintaining low self-esteem or (ii) being employed consciously to raise self-esteem.

Awareness of the emotional imagination has implications not only for individuals but for the nation and the world, for in order to create a peaceful and prosperous future we must first be able to imagine it. Yet movies depicting conditions in America one or more decades into the future show substantial escalation of violence, pollution, poverty, and anarchy. What if these celluloid scenarios represent limitations of our vision? If that is so, we need to know and understand the emotional imagination because it can be a powerful ally in the process of renewal.

When its function remains unconscious, the emotional imagination often becomes an instrument of self-torture and self-defeat. This problem is apparent in the involuntary imaginings of worst-case scenarios and other visualizations of worrisome and distressful natures. It is certainly apparent in the production of visualizations that reinforce a person's emotional conviction of his inadequacies and failures.

Those plagued by a renegade emotional imagination include worriers, cynics, perfectionists, jealous types, many kinds of phobics, shy people, and bored and depressed people. Artists and writers, journalists and scientists, actors and performers are among those whose careers and happiness can be impeded by the vagaries of the emotional imagination.

Awareness of the emotional imagination and the manners in which it becomes blocked and unblocked can mean emotional and creative salvation for millions of people. Learning about the emotional imagination means becoming more aware of why we choose to perceive what we perceive, why we imagine what we imagine, and why we feel what we are feeling.

The emotional imagination comprises both voyeurism and exhibitionism. Voyeurism is understood by laymen in the context of sex and the Peeping Tom. (A recent news magazine cover story on voyeurism described it entirely in sexual terms.) But voyeurism consists of much more than sexual matters. There exists a general condition called *negative peeping.* This consists of the human tendency to produce visual images via imagination, or the actual looking for scenes or conditions in the environment, to feed negative feelings.

For example, many of us employ the voyeuristic drive unconsciously to exaggerate our fears and imagine worst-case scenarios. One client lost $2,000 in the stock market and for weeks afterward felt like a failure. He felt this way because he became a negative peeper, an involuntary voyeur of negative scenarios and expectations, producing in his imagination distressful images of himself becoming a bum, even though he had plenty of money.

This problem of negative peeping is an unconscious compulsion in millions of people that produces bad feelings about themselves and their lives. In 99.9 percent of cases, people are not aware of how they misuse the imagination to feed their negative feelings. The negative feelings are the consequences of our unconscious inclinations to engage in looking foolish, or feeling refused, deprived, controlled, dominated, criticized, rejected, humiliated, shamed, scorned, punished, condemned, and so on. Each person's tendencies in this respect are derived from his or her childhood experiences and perceptions.

In other words, via the emotional imagination everyday "normal" people, in various degrees, seek out, promote, create, or misuse present-day external problems to resurrect feelings associated with unresolved emotional conflicts from childhood. For example, a person with anxiety about attending social events imagines that others will ignore him or look down on him, even though in reality that would not happen unless he were to behave inappropriately. Before going to a social event, he may for several days peep into the future, seeing himself at the event being seen by others in a negative light.

As a child, this person felt different, ignored, and disliked by others. As an adult, he transfers these unresolved childhood feelings of being seen as inadequate onto present events. Using the emotional imagination, he resurrects those old, unresolved feelings in the various situations of his life.

A person's emotional reality is largely based on the speculations and visualizations of his emotional imagination. One client with low self-esteem and obsessive-compulsive emotional problems had been frequently abused and even terrorized as a child by his father. As an adult, he often slipped into fearful feelings that he would be humiliated, exposed, and helpless in different situations. One Sunday in church he became convinced that the minister was going to call upon him to lead prayers and that he would be too nervous to perform. He was unlikely to be called upon because 600 people were present for the minister to choose from. Nevertheless, my client became convinced emotionally of this prospect of impending humiliation, and he got up and walked out of the church in the middle of the service. Then he felt awful about himself for being weak and out of control.

I told him, "Emotionally, you are flirting with the old feelings of being exposed and humiliated that are familiar from your past and which you still have not worked out or resolved. In the past, your father was the agent of your terror; now you yourself create the terror when an opportunity arises. You know intellectually the terror is irrational, unwarranted by the situation. But through your emotional imagination, you peep into the near future and you create a scenario in which your worst fears are being realized. In that moment, you become convinced of the validity of this way of seeing the situation."

"But it's true," he said. "I was panicking. If the minister had called upon me, I would not have been able to do well."

"Yes, at that point indeed you might have done poorly," I agreed. "But what produced that degree of anxiety? Via the emotional imagination, you begin to flirt with the prospect of being shamed and humiliated. This creates your anxiety. It feels as if these anxious or panicky feelings are grabbing you by the throat, and you believe your panic is the primary problem. But the panic is just a surface symptom. The primary problem is your continuing attachment to feelings of shame and humiliation. Your father forced you to submit to shameful experiences when you were a youngster. In church you imagined that the minister, like Dad, was going to force you into a situation that would bring up those familiar old feelings. The more you see and understand the inner operations by which you continue to look for opportunities to feel shame, the more this problem will go away."

This teaching process involves four primary areas of focus: 1) understanding the precise emotional difficulties that are unresolved from your past; 2) seeing how you have been conditioned to recreate those feelings and impressions in the context of your present life; 3) understanding how you maintain those feelings through unconscious attachments and through the emotional imagination; and 4) beginning to see and experience yourself in a positive new light.

When emotional problems are absent, peeping is positive, meaning the imagination is being used constructively. That condition prevails when a photographer peeps into his camera to capture beauty, a detective peeps around the crime scene to capture the criminal, the dentist peeps into a mouth looking for cavities to fix, a news reporter peeps into an event or situation trying to uncover truth or corruption, a psychotherapist peeps into a person's psyche to help resolve emotional conflicts and restore the emotional imagination to a positive alignment.

Awareness of negative peeping gives us important leverage in the struggle for self-esteem. Self-esteem is the measure to which our healthy and positive side prevails in the struggle between the negative and the positive. When we unconsciously pursue the negative, as in negative peeping, we're the keepers of our misery, the jailers of our souls.

Nation of Peepers

Missionaries in the rain forests of Brazil gave flashlights to the Indians. The Indians, who previously relied on hearing, smelling, and intuition to manage at night, now had technology to show them around the jungle in the dark.

By the time their batteries ran down, the Indians were dependent on the flashlights. They went back to the missionaries for more batteries and, as a trade-off, had to swallow a missionary's version of the light.

Thomas Edison, whose former winter home is up the road several miles from where I lived in Florida, invented light bulbs and made us creatures of the night. Now we are all more dependent than ever on our visual capacity, while our other senses have become less essential.

Fifty years ago, everyone tuned their ears and imaginations to radio. Now the onus is on the eyes as we gather around giant TV screens, computers, and video games as our ancestors did the fire. That taxes my eyes—I flush them once in a while in cold distilled water to soothe them.

We are not only more visual in orientation, but we also have become a nation of peepers. People peep out at the world from behind dark glasses, looking without being seen. They peep through binoculars, cameras, video cameras. Sexual peepers are consumers of dirty books and videos. Gossipers are peepers at the keyholes of life. Body-builders, silicon breast consumers, and glamorous personalities peep in anticipation of seeing people peeping back at them in admiration.

The more that we feel unsure about ourselves, the more tempted we are to peep into the lives of others in order to feel superior or to look for ways to feel deprived, controlled, criticized, rejected, and otherwise offended.

Voyeurism has always been around, but it became more important psychologically beginning in the last century when photography and the mass production of photographs began to turn ordinary people into casual peepers. When the Hindenburg dirigible exploded in 1937, the *New York Post* printed seven pages of pictures and the *New York Daily Mirror* printed nine. These days magazines such as *Time, Newsweek,* and *Life* offer up a peeper's paradise, a visual feast of events, people, and personalities, while our culture is increasingly defined and framed by images.

This is not a problem in itself. The problem lies in the fact that peeping is compulsive, negative, or self-deprecating in orientation for millions of us. Compulsive TV viewers, for instance, sit on the abyss of inertia, peeping passively into the drama of other people's lives. "Couch potato" is not an expression we associate with the best in ourselves because it signifies an inability to resist visual images, no matter how trite. As another example, peeping is compulsive and negative in racists who peep assiduously at the rainbow of humanity, desperate to spot others who they want to be more worthless than they know themselves to be.

One friend, a covert peeper, was a sharp-eyed reader of bumper stickers. He didn't realize he was looking for offense in these aphorisms until he angrily vowed to join the gun-control lobby after seeing three bumper stickers in one day that read, "God, Guts, and Guns."

We love to peep at others, as attested by the popularity of trashy biographical books on celebrities. We peeped Greta Garbo to death. The day after she died in 1990, two photographs of her appeared side-by-side in the *San Francisco Chronicle*. One photo showed the beautiful silent-film star of the 1920s; the other showed a crippled old hag huddled in her coat. We loved to look at Greta Garbo in her final agony. The tabloids paid fortunes to photographers to chase her down the street, to capture the gargoyle of her former self, so we could peep in our perverse glee, identifying with her feeling of being seen in all her ugliness.

One of my favorite peepers was a bird-watcher. She loved to camp on weekends alone on one of Florida's small deserted coastal islands and check out the bird life through her powerful binoculars. But on the mainland she was a workaholic who carried within her psyche an emotional conviction that people looking at her found her to be inadequate or unworthy.

The deserted island became her great escape. There, no eyes could look at her. No one was around to see her as she felt she was seen on the mainland—as ugly and inadequate. "I don't secretly indulge in the feeling of being looked at and judged," her inner defenses maintained. "You see how much I like it here where no one sees me. Besides, I am not passively attached to being seen critically—I am the one who does the seeing."

Another peeper I knew was a nudist. She too had a core issue involving an unconscious attachment to being seen with disapproval. She was an attractive woman who nonetheless felt her body was too fat and unappealing. At the nudist beaches, she preferred to sit in the sand, watching and evaluating others on the basis of bodies and personalities.

Whenever she stood up and walked around, however, she became very conscious of the eyes of others upon her. It felt as if they were sizing her up as unacceptable. Not surprisingly, she felt more relaxed at an inland nudist camp where older, "more forgiving" people gathered, rather than the "Club Med" style colony near Tampa where the young and beautiful congregated.

In her office, she found herself peeping at co-workers who were smoking (against company rules) and gossiping. She felt they ought to be punished. She peeped in order to identify with the feeling of being seen doing something "bad," thereby conjuring up that old familiar feeling from her own past.

In college, she had been an alcoholic and drug user, acting out the conviction that her mother, teachers, and classmates saw her as bad. Although she no longer abused substances, she still had not worked out this self-defeating attachment to being seen in a negative light.

Women peep at TV and fashion magazines to see images of "Miss Body Beautiful," the cute, slender, buxom Barbie dolls often produced by diet pills, cosmetic artistry, plastic surgery, and breast implants. As they peep, they feel more deficient and inadequate in themselves. Before the mass production of visual images, a woman was not bombarded daily with glorified images of feminine perfection. She was less tempted to be preoccupied with her size, shape, and looks. She was not as likely to be under constant inner reproach for failing to live up to these ideals.

Of course, there is nothing wrong with fashion magazines. But many of the most avid readers of those magazines are believers in the fallacy that their value is dependent on how attractively they are seen by others. The epidemics of bulimia and anorexia—eating disorders mostly involving women—are related to a cultural bias against heavy women. The modern epidemic of these disorders may therefore be associated with the mass production of visual images which stimulate women to feel more deeply their alleged unattractiveness and unworthiness. The need is to raise self-esteem so women do not "buy into" this cultural bias and can feel their own intrinsic value, independent of external values.

With men, the attachments to feeling unworthy are acted out in what are often more covert manners, primarily through emotional withdrawal, violent tempers, depression, inability to communicate feelings, as well as through addictive and compulsive behaviors. Men are wrapped up in self-image, too, and peep at their fashion magazines, dreaming of being Mr. Irresistible. Body builders and steroid users are muscle peepers whose sense of self is so undeveloped they have compensated with a caricature of masculine power. The more that a man suffers from low self-esteem, the more likely he is emotionally involved in protecting a fragile self-image.

Another client, a former drug addict, described to me the experience of out-of-control peeping on the day he had tried to kill himself with a drug overdose. "From the time I got up in the morning," he said, "I spent the day walking around in a daze, acting, talking, moving, my whole mind in this world of imagination, seeing me kill myself, rehearsing it all day long."

He was peeping into his imagination to feed on feelings of being unwanted and unloved. "I was seeing my death," he went on, "seeing friends finding my body, the funeral, the music, who came, who didn't come, who sent flowers. Not until now, with therapy, have I realized how much I was totally absorbed in the fantasy, the visualizing of it as you say. For me back then, it was real. I made it the reality. It was the only reality I was interested in."

He was no longer suicidal but still had a tendency to slip into vivid fantasies, often of a morose or perverse nature. "Boy, that was sick!" he often said to himself after snapping out of these self-defeating voyeuristic expeditions through his imagination. The common themes of his visualizations dealt with experiences of feeling unloved, a secret attachment to which his emotional imagination had become indentured.

I estimate that the average peeper spends three months of his life looking into a refrigerator, six months looking into a mirror, and six years looking into the eyes and minds of other people for disapproval and rejection.

For the most part, remember that other people are not judging you and probably not even thinking about you—they have better things to do. If you waste time comparing yourself to others, or judging yourself and others, you are attached to being seen by others as inadequate and worthless.

These attachments will ensure that you will not succeed or get what you want, further reinforcing those negative beliefs about yourself.

Negative Peeping

Let's look in more detail into the problem of peeping and its relationship to low self-esteem.

Eyes are like sponges absorbing sights and impressions. A person processes visual stimuli through the filtering system of his brain to orient himself and to survive in the world. His visual impressions produce a great variety of thoughts and feelings.

Of course, an individual does not see with pure objectivity. Human beings are born with great self-centeredness and, consequently, profound misconceptions of reality. Only gradually over many years does a person become more objective.

A person sees the world *subjectively,* meaning from his own self-centeredness. People interpret what they see according to their own personal beliefs, prejudices, fears, expectations, desires, goals, and learning. For example, a person with low self-esteem sees an admirable person and feels inferior; a person with high self-esteem sees the same person and is inspired by him.

A person with low self-esteem is a *negative peeper.* His eyes and his imagination become generators of negative images about himself, others, and the world. The problem is unconscious. The typical negative peeper does not know that control of his eyes and his imagination is under the influence of an unconscious part of himself that instigates unhappiness and self-defeat.

Negative peepers have their inner antennas on alert for evidence that they are being deprived, refused, controlled, dominated, rejected, betrayed, and criticized. They can see actual evidence of this, or they can imagine the evidence exists in what they are seeing. Or they can see the evidence with their imagination, in daydreams and visualizations, even while their eyes are closed.

They can also see or imagine the evidence even when the supposed evidence is not real. This is because it is not truth they are looking for. Their unconscious mind is looking for subjective impressions, which are then used to satisfy or affirm their right to suffer or feel hurt by the failures or actions of others.

A primary element in negative peeping is our temptation to play the role of victim in some context or other. If we could run the 100-yard dash as quickly as we spot opportunities to feel refused, deprived, controlled, criticized, and rejected, we would be built like cheetahs.

Worriers are obvious examples of negative peepers. They peer into the future and become agitated by the worst-case scenarios that their imaginations produce. It is fine to plan wisely for the future, but worriers absorb an unpleasant emotional experience *in the present moment* for what has not yet occurred and may never occur. They are specialists in idle speculations of the worst kind. They are flagrant creators of their own suffering.

Because their negative peepings are compulsive, worriers

are consequently obsessively involved with their future prospects. It may be that, given the facts, there is much for them to enjoy in the present moment. But their unconscious agendas override the facts. They are not looking for enjoyment in the present moment. Rather, they are looking for ways to recreate or replay familiar feelings of injustice, neglect, and deprivation.

Worriers rationalize that they are future-focused in order to prevent bad things from happening. But they are really future-focused in order to fulfill an unconscious agenda—that of becoming entangled emotionally in the prospect of being deprived, controlled, rejected, criticized, and so on. The consequences include anxiety, depression, and low self-esteem.

By imagining that the future holds more loss, more rejection, and more criticism, the worrier unconsciously indulges in those negative feelings in the present. For instance, a man who is constantly worried something bad will happen to his investments is entangled in a secret attachment to loss and deprivation. He is predisposed to produce unpleasant visualizations of loss, through which he remains trapped in that expectation. (Secret attachments are distasteful leftovers from childhood that produce the tendencies all of us have to become involved unconsciously in feeling deprived, refused, controlled, dominated, rejected, criticized, and so on.)

In one sense, the worrier's plight can be considered a bad habit. It is a habit which, in order to break, requires knowledge of the existence and operation of his own secret attachments to negative feelings, as well as understanding of the visual component in keeping those feelings alive.

While worriers peep into the future, others peep into the past, among them bitter men and women, cynics, and those full of regret or nostalgia. As they peep into the past, they are looking for the hurts and injustices—real or imagined—that they have endured. (Some nostalgic people may be indulging in how much they are missing out on "the good old days.") They hold onto grudges and grievances like aristocrats do the family jewels. They believe these unhappy memories account for their suffering in the present. But their suffering is attributable to their unconscious willingness to scan the past to relive old hurts and injustices.

So why do they not forget, forgive, and clean the slate? Because they are not aware of how precious their collection of grievances is to them, and because even if they were aware, they still might not be willing to let go, even knowing how much they suffer holding on.

Some people peep into the future with high hopes and great expectations and look for magic or romantic solutions to their problems. They pray, "When my ship comes in (and yes, it's there just beyond the horizon), I'll finally be happy." But they are secretly committed to self-denial in the present.

One overweight client had been looking forward for months to a friend's wedding because, "I just knew I'd show up slim and pretty and impress everyone with how well I'm doing." When the wedding day finally arrived, she was as overweight as ever and feeling reluctant to go. She was caught up in the conviction that others would be watching her and judging her as inferior. She used her weight problem as a justification to indulge in feeling rejected and looked down on. She projected forlorn fantasies beyond every new horizon, while her present was a self-created wasteland.

The typical negative peeper sees others looking back at him with his own eyes replacing theirs. He imagines what others are thinking and feeling as they look back at him. He reflects his own negative expectations off their eyes.

I remember one client, an office manager, complaining of the lack of respect he got from his assistant manager. But when this client looked into the eyes or the face of his assistant, he expected to see that disrespect coming back at him. In fact, my client gave off subliminal messages in his own eyes and face that reflected that expectation. So he got what he was looking for. His assistant knew it, too, albeit unconsciously, and played into what was expected of him. It is in such secret collusions that we experience our worst fears and bring out the worst in each other.

When we "fall in love" with another person, we are reacting in part to the reflection of ourselves in the eyes of the "beloved." We see in those eyes the confirmation of all our virtues. That full and unqualified acceptance of ourselves feels like heaven, for now we have this defense against our harsh inner voice, "I am not worthless and no good; see how much I am adored in my beloved's eyes."

However, the lover is loving himself, his own idealized self, that he sees reflected and adored in the eyes of his beloved. If the couple fails to get beyond the initial infatuation into deeper or more mature love, the bloom fades from the romance and those same eyes narrow and harden with disappointment.

Often a negative peeper is afraid of public speaking. He is reluctant to look at all those faces and is even more anxious about looking into all those eyes, because he sees in those faces various expressions of doubt about his own worth. Those faces and eyes threaten to overwhelm him, even to annihilate him, with their alleged rejection, lack of interest, and suggestion that he is unworthy. If in reality a negative reaction is *not* there in those faces, he will imagine it is anyway. He succumbs to the force of this imagined disapproval coming at him, and he is nervous to the point that he fails to do well.

Injustice Collecting

Injustice collecting is also an expression of low self-esteem. Injustice collecting and negative peeping go together like tag-team wrestlers.

The injustice collector is a skilled peeper. He has an inner eye that scans the environment for possible opportunities to feel criticized, rejected, and denied. Visually, he zooms in on real or imagined negative elements and feeds on the hurt of it all. He could be marching down Main Street in the Fourth of July parade, his brass buttons all polished and his heart in heaven, when he spots an old enemy in the crowd. For the next several minutes—if not several hours—his unconscious spews out images of how he was a victim of that person, and he feels the torment all over again.

His anger at or hatred for the perceived injustice is not for the purpose of resolving the problem. Rather his anger defends against his secret willingness to indulge in feeling victimized. Meanwhile, without realizing it, he will provoke the rejection and insults on which he feeds.

Bill had raised injustice collecting to an art. Misery followed him everywhere, like an ugly mutt running down the highway after his master's car. He was driving down the Tamiami Trail (from Tampa to Miami) when he came up behind a slow Cadillac in the fast lane. He hated waiting in doctors' offices, in supermarket lines, and especially behind stragglers with northern license tags. He knew this was an opportunity for a binge of sweet suffering. He knew but he could not resist.

He grumbled for several minutes as he nestled up to this guy's back bumper, then slipped around the slow-poke on the inside lane. Now the road was clear ahead. He gunned the engine and cruised along at a cozy ten miles above the speed limit. Free at last.

Wait a minute. He was still upset at the slow driver or, as he put it, "that idiot who has the nerve to drive slow in the fast lane." Into his side-view mirror he peeped, and he saw the Caddy way back there holding up more drivers in the passing lane.

That made him even more angry. "Why don't the cops arrest those jerks for driving slow," he thought. "They're just as dangerous as speeders and twice as stupid. Look at all those drivers behind him who he's holding up."

He continued to peep, straining to see how many cars were trapped behind the Caddy, muttering dark oaths, his eyes glinting with malice. Suddenly, a big bug splattered as a yellow splotch on Bill's windshield. Something in the configuration of the bug's remains brought him to his senses, and he said to himself, "Wow, have I ever been speeding emotionally!"

An insight struck him like the bug that hit the windshield. He realized even after passing that slow car and having the road to himself, he had continued to feel extremely negative, as if he were still being delayed. Of course, he now saw, he had been identifying with the drivers of the cars behind the Caddy, imagining them being as upset at the slow driver as he had been. In that covert manner, he had been willing to continue feeling held back.

I too have collected my share of injustices. I was "sneaking it in" when my wife Sandra and I became co-leaders of therapy groups in 1980. When Sandra was speaking, I would peep at group members in order to see them (or imagine them) being more intrigued and captivated with Sandra's insights and personality than with mine.

Several times after a group session had ended, I berated her for taking over the group and denying me time for my two cents. The more I peeped in those groups at Sandra excelling, the more I became tangled up in my own passivity, and the more likely I was to be less dynamic and effective. The feeling was pure low self-esteem.

As well as blaming Sandra, I also blamed myself for being too stiff and formal. But it was my passivity—my attachment to being seen as unworthy and unrecognized, and my willingness to indulge in those feelings—that instigated my problem. Years passed before I became aware of these secret attachments and the clever game I played unconsciously to keep them under wraps.

It is interesting to watch others collect injustices. Some time ago I was golfing in a foursome of men. We whisked around the front nine without delay, but on the back nine we came up behind two foursomes of women. Two of the men immediately began to have emotional reactions. One kept peeping up ahead, saying several times in dismay, "Look, there's a hole ahead of them. Where's that ranger? He should speed them up!"

This fellow was my partner in a little wager, and his game began to suffer. "No fun, no fun anymore," he sighed several times. On the tee at the eighteenth hole, he groaned as he peered up the fairway, "Those women ruined my day!"

"That's nothing," bellowed his fellow sufferer. "Women have ruined my life!"

I laughed, fascinated at how people can extract misery from all the prerequisites of fun and joy.

Remember, peeping is a dysfunction of the emotional imagination, and it is done to serve our unconscious attachments to perceived injustices that involve feeling deprived, controlled, rejected, and so on. These attachments are very strong and will persist even as an individual becomes aware of them.

Alice too had hungry eyes for injustices. Her parents had visited her the previous weekend, she told me in a session. "My dad was awful," she complained. "He was in town looking at some real estate. He was so wrapped up in himself and his business deals. He hardly spoke to me the whole weekend."

In questioning her, I found out that she had hovered around him all weekend, despite his indifference toward her. She had watched him closely, waiting for any crumbs of attention he might throw her way.

"There's a lot of visual mischief going on," I said. "Your eyes follow your father around, and you become preoccupied with him. You watch him moving around in his own little world of self-interest for one reason only—to deepen your sense of emotional impoverishment, to indulge in the feeling of not being recognized or appreciated by him.

"If you were not looking for this feeling, you would leave your father alone when he is not relating well to you, or at least you would not follow him around with your eyes. You would go and talk to your mom and have fun with her. Instead, however, you are willing to become preoccupied with his presence and the degree to which he's not attentive to you. So begin to try to catch yourself using your eyes in this self-defeating way, and you will discover how much more at ease you can feel when he is around."

Another injustice collector told me in a session, "I would like to learn to scuba dive, to have fun, and meet more men. But I'm afraid of sharks. I'm afraid of getting bitten." She was having difficulty establishing a relationship, and had felt in her previous relationships to have been the victim of men's rejection and lack of commitment.

"Maybe you see men as sharks," I suggested.

"Maybe I do. I do feel like a piece of meat around them. I remember going fishing a while back, and I felt so bad for the live fish we used for bait. Isn't that identifying with the victim, identifying with the shark bait?"

"Yes it is," I agreed. "There are indeed men out there who are hungry and cruel. But you are projecting this expectation onto all men. Moreover, with your mentality, you will either avoid men completely or you will make your nightmares come true by being attracted to men who, in the guise of friendly dolphins, are the most voracious sharks of all.

"You want to understand your peeping and your injustice collecting. You are unconsciously willing to see the worst in men, even before you really know a certain individual, in order to validate your victim mentality and deprive yourself of commitment and love."

My client Jerry was another graduate of the Injustice Collector's School of Misery, majoring in negative peeping. In a session, he described to me an incident at his bank. As he was standing in line to deposit his week's receipts, his patience began to sizzle because of the slowpoke commercial depositers in line in front of him.

He was seventh in line, but three depositors ahead of him were huddling with the three tellers, as if conspiring to keep him waiting. His eyes burned into the backs of their heads to no avail. Not a single teller looked up to cast a little sympathy his way.

Dark thoughts and morbid feelings clashed with his best intentions. He stewed in the juices of creeping negativity. Finally, a new trio of balky depositors moved forward. But they were soon mired in some mathematical morass with the

tellers. From Jerry's vantage in the line, the three others waiting in front of him looked distinctly like more robbers of his
precious time. He could take the abuse no longer, and he
marched out of the bank with a grumble of disgust.

It turned out, however, he might have suffered less if he
had remained waiting in the bank. For the next two hours he
continued to produce images and fantasies associated with the
futile wait, seeing the distinct nonchalance in every teller's
face and the uncaring backsides of a thousand depositors.

In his involuntary visualizations, he marched into the bank a
dozen times to close his account in protest, relishing the
contrite expressions and futile apologies of the bank employees. His imagination had no off-switch. His mind had a life of
its own. He saw the drama of his protest replayed in scores of
new scripts, some X-rated for their violence and vulgarity, and
still his mind played on. Someone with high self-esteem, however, would not repeatedly produce scenes in which he would
be seen with scorn and disgust.

Jerry's involuntary visualizations only kept alive his anger
and anxiety. The event was over and he knew intellectually he
ought to forget it. It had been no one's fault, just unfortunate
timing on his part. So why was he dwelling on the event and
continuing to suffer?

"Like everyone else," I told him, "you generate your own
unconscious process of self-torture. The extent of your negative
feelings depends on the degree of unresolved issues from your
childhood.

"We know from what you have told me of your past that you
often felt held up and held back, which is a feeling of being
controlled and forced to submit to someone else's needs and
priorities. Remember how upset you were when your parents
made you wait an extra year to get your driver's licence."

"Don't remind me," Jerry answered.

"But you are continually reminding yourself. You did it in

the bank. You are conditioned to go back into that feeling of being held up or delayed whenever an opportunity presents itself. In other words, some person or situation will be used as a catalyst to ressurect those old feelings. This process is unconscious. All you were aware of was your angry reaction to the feeling."

"If I hated it so much, why did I experience it?"

"You have a secret attachment to feeling held back. This causes you to take it personally whenever that appears to be happening, and you quickly become offended. Your anger is a defense that blocks from your awareness the degree to which you unconsciously collude in the experience of feeling held back or delayed. One reaction to the feeling of being forced to wait is your desire for immediate gratification, often observed in your ice-cream binges. So your anger is a defense which says, in effect, 'I'm not passively attached to waiting. Look how much I hate it.'

"The unpleasant visualizations you experienced after the bank wait were being served up by your unconscious to feed your attachment to being held up. As you have been learning, there is a side of ourselves that is very powerful and subversive which accounts for the self-defeating and self-destructive elements of human nature. Though people are able to grasp this intellectually, there is much resistance to seeing it on a personal level."

"Quick, tell me some good news!"

"You know what that is. You can work this out. By making conscious what has been unconscious, you can overcome this inner tyranny and liberate yourself. This goal makes living more of an adventure and gives you a heroic purpose for your life."

"Sign me up for another week," he said. "I like my starring role in *The Adventures Of Inner Space*."

Figments of Imagination

So what are you looking for with your eyes? Often you are looking for some way to feel inadequate.

A shy or vain person who compulsively looks at himself in the mirror is expecting to be disappointed with what he sees. A person who lusts after bikini-clad beauties or strapping hunks on the beach may be entertaining the feeling of what he or she is not good enough to get.

A popular preoccupation is to look into the eyes of others in order to see them looking back at you with your own eyes. That means you see them looking back at you with what you imagine they are thinking or feeling about you. Your impression is based on the degree to which you are focused on or self-conscious of your own alleged weaknesses and short-comings, and how you imagine that those alleged weaknesses are exposed for all to see.

The peeper reacts to what he sees with a wide range of emotions. He may feel shy, embarrassed, or shamed and even blush. Or he may decide he does not like the person looking back at him, because he has decided that person is judgmental.

He may decide the other person is less than himself, or superior to himself, based not on facts but on his own projections. Despite these projections, he is convinced that he is an objective observer of reality.

Or he may become intrigued with and attracted to the other person, as his unconscious picks up subliminal clues that indicate this person is someone with whom he can act out all his repressed conflicts and secret attachments.

What else can you see in another person? How about projecting onto him or her certain repressed elements of your own psyche. For instance, if you are a selfish person (the result of your unconscious attachment to feeling deprived and refused), you will be quick to spot any selfish trait in the other person and immediately to dislike that person for it. This operation is the essence of "personality clashes" and is often the primary contributor to one's enemy list.

The unreliability of witnesses in court cases is well known and illustrates how we see according to unconscious variables. Discrepancies in estimates of duration, distance, background, and sizes are common among witnesses of the same event. A witness's memory is influenced by his prejudices, fears, wishes, and unconscious biases. He may have concentrated on one aspect of a crime scene to the exclusion of other important aspects. He may disregard what is unfamiliar and supplement what he actually saw with what he believes must have happened. Fact and imagination can become indistinguishable if his pride gets in the way and he believes his self-importance hinges on the quality of his memory, or if he puts his self-image ahead of the accuracy of his observations.

One's personality is an adaptation to compensate for unconscious conflicts. For example, the perfectionist sees a world full of critics, judges, and evaluators. His perfectionism is his defense against his expectation of being criticized. Much of the energy of his emotional imagination is wasted in fantasies in which he sees and feels himself being criticized by others. His emotional energy is also consumed in the rationalizations and visualizations he creates in order to defend against this secret attachment.

The jealous person is expecting to be rejected, and he conjures up images of his spouse or lover betraying him. The images he produces leave him uncertain about reality and intensify his poor feelings about himself.

Jealousy is not just simple peeping but the result of infantile resignation to the feeling of having been excluded from a relationship with one or both parents. The jealous person is always trying to "prove" that his imaginings are an exact reconstruction of the facts. In any case, his peeping is incidental to the real problem—his attachment to rejection.

One woman had been torturing herself daily for more than a year with visualizations of her husband making love to his secretary. However, her husband was kind, loyal, and devoted to her. In spite of his reassurances to her, she continued to imagine that he was betraying her. Her problem was her expectation of (and attachment to) rejection and betrayal, stemming from her childhood when she perceived that her father favored her younger sister over her. She had transferred this unresolved conflict onto her husband.

The greedy person is expecting to be deprived, denied, or lose out on something or other, and many of his visualizations are grim scenarios depicting this outcome. Even if he had millions in the bank, he would find ways to experience deprival and loss—perhaps through poor relationships, feeling unrecognized, being bored, or bad investments.

The people-pleaser, another low self-esteem personality, also conjures up scenes of his rejection, abandonment, and disapproval by others. He does whatever it takes to gain the acceptance and approval of others. But because he is so ingratiating, others do not respect him and soon his worst fears come true.

The bored person is always looking for misery. Boredom has as its primary components an inhibition of the emotional imagination (a blockage against being creative and seeing beauty) and an attachment to being refused. Despite his existence in a dynamic and thrilling world, the bored person is like a magician able to create feelings of emptiness and nothingness out of thin air. The feeling may be, "There is nothing here for me—because I am no good and deserve this fate!"

When a person is chronically bored, he becomes preoccupied, even obsessed, with what he believes he is *not* getting. A primary experience for him is the absence of good feelings about himself. In constrast, someone who feels good about himself may experience occasional boredom—but mostly he feels that life is fulfilling.

One type of bored person is the chronic complainer who in his complaining is passive-aggressively asserting, "I'm not looking for the feeling of nothing. The problem is, there is nothing on this plate (in this world) that interests me." He lets you know how unhappy he is about that, as he unconsciously but purposely declines to see or appreciate the beauty and pleasure the world has to offer.

Another type of bored person is the frantic funseeker, who in his hectic and often futile search for fun betrays the behind-the-scenes presence of his boredom. He is more likely to experience distracted agitation than fun.

Boredom is often a passing feeling, unpleasant but harmless enough. But for millions of people it is a chronic emotional problem that can have significant social impact. For example, bored people may be more likely to speculate or gamble on financial markets to compensate for their inner inertia, thereby destabilizing the economy. Some of them will promote violence or war for the sake of excitement. Boredom promotes economic loss from lack of creativity and enthusiasm. It heightens the appeal of drugs and alcohol, promiscuity and criminality. It weakens democracy through indifference to political and social processes.

Antidotes to boredom include fantasy, hobbies, entertainment, and work. Fantasy, or imagination in free flight, is visual. People with a neurotic inhibition of fantasy (writer's or artist's block, for instance) are likely to experience chronic boredom. The inhibition is related to conflicts over early childhood prohibitions against peeping (see chapters, "Seeing Into Shyness" and "Forbidden Sights"). In other words, the inner conscience will veto the use of fantasy on the grounds that it constitutes forbidden peeping.

Boredom can also be an unconscious defense to ward off self-aggression, which in the form of inner voices looks for incriminating material to punish the individual. This defense consists of clearing all incriminating material from the psychic chambers, leaving them empty. It is like the mystery novel ruse where the corpse is removed before the police arrive. The bored person goes a step further, denying that the premises could have anything in them, even at some future date. For this defense, the person may neutralize the self-aggression, but a life of boredom ("I get nothing") and low self-esteem is his end of this devil's bargain.

Celebrity Peeping

Whenever the average person spots a celebrity in the flesh, he has an emotional reaction that usually varies according to his self-esteem and also the degree to which the celebrity is famous.

If the celebrity you see is the local TV weatherman, your eyes might soak him or her up for an instant or two, and then you will go about your business with a minimum of emotional disruption.

However, if the celebrity is a high-flying Hollywood movie star, your eyes fasten like rivets to his or her body and, depending on your self-esteem, you could be instantly transported into an altered consciousness complete with rapid pulse and sweaty palms.

The lower your own self-esteem, the greater will be your emotional thrill in being in the presence of a celebrity. The cult of the celebrity is a cultural anomaly that flourishes under the auspices of the low self-esteem of the masses. Your self-esteem is also inversely proportional to the time you spend fantasizing about being a celebrity.

Within the cult of celebrity, fame matters more than substance. A celebrity's validation by the culture, not our own personal judgment of his worth, determines his status in our eyes. If Benedict Arnold returned to modern America in a blaze of media attention, it is probable that millions of people would want to shake his hand and stand bedazzled in his presence. It is not the possibility of reincarnation that would be exciting them but the emotional thrill of feeling their own selves being observed, noticed, and perhaps even acknowledged by someone deemed a VIP.

Since the typical person feels his own value only to a relative degree, he relishes any emotional surges of good feelings about himself. A celebrity's notice of him (or the prospect that a celebrity will at any moment notice him) makes the average person feel that he counts for something other than his everyday anonymity. One of my clients said his main claim to fame was a three-day drunk he passed with a famous stuntman.

Just about everyone has shortcomings of self-esteem. Even successful and prominent people at times inwardly reproach themselves for alleged failures, inadequacy, even worthlessness, while entangled in their psyches' fears and dissatisfactions. How many times has a movie star's inner conscience tormented him for not being more famous? Under that accusation, this movie star would feel grateful for the fans cheering him as he walked into the opening night showing of his latest big hit. "You see," his defenses could say to his mocking inner conscience or super-ego, "you're wrong—I am somebody important. Look how many people recognize my value."

Just about everyone is under some degree of accusation from his inner conscience to the effect that he is unimportant and insignificant. A person with low self-esteem is often bullied by his inner conscience, "You won't amount to anything! You're always screwing up! You're a loser! And everybody knows it!"

To compensate, it is convenient to identify with celebrities, to imagine what it would be like to be in the shoes of one VIP or another. This can provide a satisfactory defense for our attachments to feeling inadequate and worthless. "This is how I would like to be!" proclaims the inner defense. "This is how I would like to feel! This is what I want for myself!"

Put another way, most of us labor under the feeling of not being recognized for who we are and what we do. So when we stand in the presence of a celebrity, we not only rub shoulders with him, we rub psyches, eager to pick up some of the magical omnipotence of someone whose self-importance is exposed for all neurotics to see and admire. "You see, this is what I really would like," we plea in our unconscious defense." I'm tired feeling like a worthless, unknown nobody."

Everything is relative. Surely there is at least one person who spent his leisure hours watching *Lifestyles of the Rich and Famous*, bemoaning his poor humdrum life, who then flew off on vacation to a Third World country where the natives gawked at him and envied this rich American because he came from the Land of Oz.

I saw my first celebrity at age fourteen. Not a lot of them showed up in the north woods where I lived, but one day I walked into our jukebox hangout and saw Little Beaver, a midget wrestler, sitting on a stool sipping a milkshake. I scampered across the street, plunked down my chocolate sundae money for a pen and pad, and hurried back for his autograph. It may have been the only one he gave out that day, but he got me high without my sugar boost.

We know from biographies that some of the most famous people in America—Marilyn Monroe, Ernest Hemingway, Janis Joplin, and thousands more—suffered from low self-esteem and other emotional problems. Yet the rest of us have held them up as paragons of success, and dreamed forlornly of one day being good enough to follow in their steps.

We not only exalt celebrities, but we love to peep at their trials and tribulations. It feels so good to see a celebrity suffer. That way we do not feel so bad about not being a celebrity. We manage temporarily to neutralize the inner conscience attack that scolds us with, "How come you're not as smart and well-known as that person." To see a celebrity unravel before our eyes provides us with the sour-grapes defense, "Look, you see what's happening to him. See how pathetic he is. Who says I should be like him."

The process does not have to involve celebrities. I read recently in *People* magazine about a 41-year-old man who shot himself in the head and died only minutes after he had shot his 18-year-old son to death in a hunting accident. What purpose does it serve to give this private tragedy a two-page spread? It is because people love to read this stuff. "Boy, it's nice not to have it that bad," they say thankfully to themselves, or, "You think I screw up—well, not nearly as bad as that!"

When I was a kid and watched *The Mousekeeters* on television, I remember asking myself, "How come I'm not one of the kids on that show? Am I not good enough for Mickey Mouse?" Deep down I felt I wasn't. The media and their visual images now provide a thousand chances a day to compare ourselves unfavorably with others. This is a radical change from 100 years ago. The consequences of this change can be positive, a leap in self-awareness and subsequent appreciation of our essence, our own intrinsic value.

In psychoanalytic language, celebrities are personifications of our ego-ideal. The ego-ideal is the grandiose version of ourselves formed in childhood when our megalomania or extreme self-centeredness is most pronounced. Naive childhood beliefs—such as "I'll be president (or great at something) when I grow up"—illustrate the essence of this idealized self.

So we project our own idealized self onto celebrities. They

are what we would like to be. We see in them our idealized self. Later in life, our inner conscience is always ready to torture us with criticism and reproach when our lives do not measure up to the expectations of our idealized self. When we "buy into" the negative messages of that impersonal, even alien, side of ourselves, we believe the worst about ourselves and feel like lonely nobodies. Then celebrities seem to us like gods.

Negative Exhibitionism

The woman on *America's Funniest Home Videos* was climbing out of a boat onto a dock. Suddenly she looked up, apparently surprised to see herself being filmed. She began to totter on the edge of the dock, collapsed back into the boat, and completed a back roll across the seat of the boat into the water.

She came out of the water sputtering for breath and covering her face with embarrassment. I gave her an A for negative exhibitionism.

Whenever a person is feeling self-conscious (a direct expression of low self-esteem), he is apt to exhibit negatively. When the woman saw the camera on her, she felt immediately self-conscious, and she began to imagine (peep) that she was being seen (and would continue being seen, since she was being filmed) in a negative light.

Her unconscious defenses now covered up her attachment to being seen negatively with a claim to power: "I cause it to happen. People see me this way because I do dumb things."

As she stumbled and tumbled into the water, she indeed caused herself to be seen in certain light, although not so much negative as hilarious.

She came out of the water embarrassed for having acted foolish, but successfully having defended against her passive attachment to being seen negatively ("I caused it to happen"). However, she may have suffered for some time with embarrassment, although good-natured laughter from her friends must have eased the pain somewhat. In any case, the experience did nothing for her self-esteem.

The emotional imagination, as stated earlier, comprises both voyeurism and exhibitionism. Often the one exhibiting is unconsciously identifying with the one who is peeping. Fashion models, singers, and actors exhibit. So do writers with their words, musicians with their music, and athletes who perform in front of teammates and spectators.

Exhibiting takes on a negative connotation when it is being used as a defense to cover up peeping. For example, the sports "choker" is a negative exhibitor. Unconsciously, he is expecting others to see him as a failure, and he carries in his psyche a secret attachment to the feeling of being seen in this light. To cover this up, he will make a claim to power: "I'm seen negatively not because of my attachment to that feeling, but because I cause it to happen by choking and falling apart."

He says, "Oh, I want to win so badly. Look how nervous I am. That proves how much I want to win and be seen with respect and approval by others." But unconsciously he is eager to act out being seen as a loser.

One negative exhibitionist, a tennis player, would easily beat his playing buddies in practice, but choke and be defeated by them in tournaments. I gave him this negative mantra to say, and it enabled him to play as well in tournaments as he did in practice: "Oh, isn't this wonderful! Won't it just make my day to step out on the court and be defeated by this guy! Isn't that what I'm secretly looking for. Wouldn't I like my friends in the stands to see me get beaten by this guy. Won't that just make my day!"

This mantra brought into his awareness the unconscious game of self-defeat, thereby diffusing the tendency to act out secret defeatist tendencies.

Defenses are intended to demonstrate some form of psychic innocence, hence defenses are dramatized *exhibitionistic* demonstrations. A person's defense, before it is acted upon, is initially a counter-claim to the inner conscience, saying, "I'm not guilty of the crime you accuse me of. To prove it, I'm going to show you what it is I really did or want." Thus, exhibitionism becomes a "big shot" in the psychic landscape. However, voyeurism is an original drive, while exhibitionism is a subsequent defense.

In the realms of unconscious accounting, peeping is "worse" than exhibiting. For example, a man attached to the feeling of being seen as a failure might plead in his defense, "No, the problem is I have no personality and I provoke people." However, he now feels bad about himself for the "lesser crime" of being without personality, and he is deceived by this defense into believing that lack of personality is his major problem—when it is in fact only a symptom of his underlying attachment to the feeling of being a failure.

The negative exhibitionist, then, is displaying for the world to see that he is indeed guilty—but only of the lesser crime of exhibitionism.

From the problem of jealousy comes a straightforward example of negative exhibitionism or, to be colloquial, making an ass of yourself. The jealous person peeps at his girlfriend looking at another man and, later, he conjures up imaginary scenes of her "making out" with this guy. His unconscious "crime" is to feast on the visualizations, feeding his secret attachments to rejection and betrayal. Meanwhile, as he peeps he becomes convinced he is entitled to his suspicions.

Now he may parade around proclaiming to all the injustice of his predicament and the lack of commitment on his girlfriend's part. The more he exhibits in an angry, hostile manner, the more he will be overreacting and drawing attention to himself. Soon he will feel guilty and upset at himself for his overreaction and, as an alternative to blaming his girlfriend or the other fellow, he may begin to be convinced that he is foolish or weak or undesirable (or whatever other lesser "crimes" his defenses may plead guilty to).

The individual will now feel guilty, shamed, or depressed for the lesser crime—the negative exhibitionism. In order to make this defense work, he has to suffer for whatever he has pleaded guilty to—being weak, foolish, selfish, distrusting, etc. The suffering takes the form of guilt, shame, depression, self-doubt, anxiety, low self-esteem, and so on.

One client became aware of the degree to which he imagined himself exhibiting inappropriately if he tried to take an unpopular stand on a management issue. He was a supervisor who had come up from the ranks and who was expected by his superiors to turn down a request made by a group of workers. In the meeting to inform the workers, the supervisor "caved in" under the pressure of the workers and compromised with them in a way that upset his superiors. His decision led to repercussions when his compromise had to be overruled in favor of the company. The client said in his session, "I just felt that if I was firm and said no, they would see me as an arrogant bastard who sided with management and who didn't care at all about them anymore. I just couldn't stand the feeling of them seeing me that way."

The man had been convinced that to be tough and do his job would be exhibiting himself negatively—being seen as inappropriate in the eyes of the workers. The irony is that an impartial observer of that meeting would have seen the supervisor in a positive light if he had carried through diplomatically and firmly with what had been expected of him. The workers also would have understood he was only doing what his job required, and would not have necessarily taken a stand against him personally.

But the supervisor had been caught in powerful feelings of being seen as arrogant, unfriendly, and a lackey of management. He had been convinced he was being forced into being "an arrogant bastard" and was consumed with guilt for taking such an unpopular stance. He focused on his alleged inappropriateness (exhibitionism) as his problem. This covered up his deeper problem, which was peeping—looking in the eyes of the workers for the feeling of being rejected by them.

My son Matthew used to get tangled up in negative exhibitionism in somewhat the way I have—though to a lesser degree than myself. He started golfing with me when he was twelve and quickly discovered how difficult it is to hit that cursed little ball, let alone in the right direction.

He was uncomfortable playing with strangers, but even playing alone with me he became downcast after a certain quota of whiffs, duffed grounders, and pop-ups into the palmettos. Some people would say that, under such circumstances, his feelings of frustration were normal. The point is, he did not have to suffer emotionally. The suffering was a result of the degree to which he began to reproach himself for doing it wrong, which was a result of his claim to power (to focus on, "I cause it to happen") to cover up his attachment to being seen as inadequate.

Once he focused on causing it to happen, he was obliged to feel bad for his alleged incompetence. (This unconscious operation is complicated and tricky to understand, which accounts for why people do not see through the defense.)

In any case, as his mood deteriorated, it was hard for me to resist becoming annoyed with him. "We're just here to have fun, Matt," I encouraged him. "Don't worry so much about results." But that did not always perk him up.

I have played with many golfers who have been eager to torture themselves because their shots did not go where they were "supposed to." Watching these self-sufferers hardly bothers me now because I hold quite firmly to my pleasure. But Matthew's funky mood did bother me. The more it bothered me, the more he was aware of that, and the worse he played, which was his negative exhibitionism.

My frustration developed because I had identified with Matthew and had imagined how he felt being looked at as incompetent or inadequate. I identified with him because of my own secret willingness to get tangled up in these feelings and because, being my son, my inclination to identify with him was more powerful than with a friend or stranger.

To repeat the tricky part again, Matthew covered up his peeping (seeing me and others looking at him with disapproval for flubbing up or imagining that we disapproved) by claiming that, in his "bad" play, *he had caused us* to look at him with disapproval. He believed he was guilty of bad golf and did not see his attachment to being judged negatively. If he were guilty of bad golf, as his defense contended, he was obliged to experience punishment (self-reproach) for playing badly, and to act out with frustration and anger. The more this defense was employed, the more he would be convinced that bad play and his angry reactions were his primary rather than secondary problems.

He understands when I explain how this works, and he seems to be less hampered by this emotional difficulty.

In summary, exhibitionism is a manner to provoke or to defend against inner feelings of being worthless, beaten out by others, scorned, and humiliated. The more a person exhibits as a reaction to these feelings, the more he sets himself up to be scorned and rejected.

More Ways to Feel Bad

I first became aware of the significance of the visual drive about seven years ago. I had gone to a furniture store looking for a lounge chair. A salesman approached me and, like all good salesman, tried to take over my will.

Now, salesmen have indeed done so in the past. I remember being mesmerized by a merchant in a rug store in New York City. This guy belonged in New York, in the major leagues. I had gone there to buy my wife a $50 Yoga mat and came away with a $3,000 Chinese silk carpet which, since I did not have the money to buy it, was purchased with installments on my credit card. The carpet lays in my office to this day. I keep my mistakes in sight in order to keep them to a minimum. At least I got the Yoga mat for free.

This time, in the furniture store, I was determined to resist the spell of the salesman. To steel myself, I must have projected my own reactive aggression upon him, for I soon felt negativity coming back from him. Discouraged by this negative charge between us, I headed for the exit. But ten feet from the door, I turned my head back over my shoulder and spied the salesman walking along behind and glaring at me like a wolf stalking a turkey.

Sure enough, out in the parking lot I began to feel like a turkey, which is of course the combined sense of being a dud, a loser, and a nobody. For hours that day I was unable to shake off that feeling. A few days later I talked about it with my analyst.

We determined that I had indeed peeped at that moment, unconsciously looking for that glare of disapproval and even scorn coming back at me from the salesman. I know the look well, going back to my parents, my sisters, and my teachers.

I had suffered again with it because of my unconscious willingness to indulge in feeling disapproved of and scorned, and I rationalized with a claim to power, to the effect that I had caused the salesman to look at me that way because of some foolishness or inadequacy in me that was apparent to him. In making that claim, I was stuck with feeling bad for my alleged shortcomings.

I had peeped, unconsciously on purpose, to experience what I had sensed would be available from the salesman—the look on his face of disapproval and scorn.

When I was a kid, I remember my younger sisters doing their Highland Flings and ballet twirl-abouts on stage at Christmas and in the living room at home. Even more than the dancing, I was captivated by the expressions of beaming satisfaction on my parents' faces. I studied their faces as if determined to measure just how much affection and approval my sisters were getting and I was *not getting*. As I peeped, my attachments to feeling unworthy and unappreciated were having a fling of their own.

A client of mine also had peeped at her parents and her sister. A real-estate agent, Nancy had become extremely anxious after only two weeks into her new job. Another woman who had joined the firm at the same time had already sold a condominium and had high hopes for another quick sale. However, Nancy had no good prospects.

Her anxiety intensified as she began to imagine that her boss was comparing her unfavorably with the other saleswoman. Nancy was obsessed with this feeling that everyone in the firm had begun to see her as inadequate.

She had a twin sister who, in Nancy's words, "was more independent and popular than I ever was." Her sister, Nancy said, "had more friends, was more of a leader. She could take over in a situation and make decisions. I felt I wasn't my own person when she was around. I felt I wasn't even worth knowing. However, I did feel like a person when I was away from her. I was glad when we no longer lived in the same city."

Based on this childhood experience, Nancy was stuck with the tendency to compare herself unfavorably with others, especially a woman competitor. Any time a boyfriend had looked at another woman, Nancy became aroused with the feeling of being less than and inadequate. She had many unnecessary fights with boyfriends who, in her peeping, she "caught" looking at other women.

At her new real-estate job, she was transferring this unresolved conflict onto the other saleswoman and using the other woman's initial success as a means to indulge in those old familiar feelings of being not good enough. The more that Nancy saw the other woman succeed, the more she felt diminished.

The visual component concerns the degree to which Nancy would *imagine* others *seeing* her as inadequate, and how she was unconsciously *looking* for signs in their *eyes* of such disapproval, as well as *watching* the other woman to *see* her doing better than herself.

Her anxiety was a consequence of her urgent need to "prove" that she was not secretly attached to this feeling.

"Look at how much I hate the feeling of being seen as inadequate," her defense would insist. "See how anxious this makes me. If only I was doing better. Then I would feel just great."

A week later, Nancy sold a unit and did indeed feel great. And because she was working out the issue in therapy, she did not go out looking for other ways to feel inadequate and less than others. She was learning to see how she contributed to her emotional difficulties.

Sometimes a person with low self-esteem overvalues his accomplishments to compensate for feelings of inadequacy. One client received numerous regional and state awards for professional competence, in part because he was so dedicated to entering every possible competition, and he had covered two walls in his office with these plaques and certificates. He had a rush of anxiety after he overheard two colleagues make sarcastic comments about his "self-booster mania." Others were seeing through his defense of overvaluation, and that generated anxiety because it confirmed his own sense of unworthiness.

Another client peeped in her new boyfriend's diary and came away with a bad case of the blues. "I couldn't resist looking, although I tried," she explained. "Now I wish I had left the diary alone. But it was too tempting when he just forgot it there in my apartment."

She discovered in the diary two columns that he had written out, one listing her good points and the other her flaws. "Naturally, I was most intrigued by the negative stuff," she admitted.

She was particularly upset by his notations that her parents had been divorced, that she was tall, and that she had "thin hair." Within minutes of reading this, she was feeling guilty and depressed.

These unpleasant reactions were products of the degree to which she took his observations as criticism and rejection of her and the degree to which she began to indulge in feeling criticized and rejected by him. However, she had not realized that this was the source of her suffering. Instead, she attributed her suffering to her "naughtiness," and her accompanying guilt and shame, for reading his diary.

"I can see now," she said, "that I was looking for something juicy and upsetting. The good stuff he wrote hardly interested me at all."

She did not tell her boyfriend she had peeped. The next evening he unexpectedly complimented her hair, perhaps out of guilt for what he had written in his diary or possibly because he suspected she had read it. Of course, she remembered his "thin hair" observation and she barely choked back a sarcastic reply that would have exposed her secret peeping.

Another client, Ruth, also had a peeping problem involving feeling rejected and unloved. She came into my office upset that her boyfriend's five-year-old daughter had come to live with them for the summer. "I guess I'm jealous of her," Ruth said. "She's so possessive of her father. She's always squeezing in between us when we hug or kiss. He even lets her sleep between us at night in our bed. In his eyes, she's perfect; she can do no wrong."

Ruth had been with her boyfriend for five years, enduring a minimum of affection and commitment from him. "I don't know that he loves me," she said. "Sometimes he asks me what I'm doing with him. I think he loves me, and he doesn't know it. He's not sure, he doesn't quite believe it yet."

Ruth's mother, who died when Ruth was sixteen, was an alcoholic "who never wanted me," Ruth said. She had lived with her father following a divorce when she was three. "My mother tried to make me hate my father," she said. "My mother believed that the world was against her and that nobody loved her or cared about her. Mom never remarried or even had a steady boyfriend."

Ruth had identified with her mother's feelings of being unloved and unwanted. Now as an adult, she was secretly willing to be involved with a man who was ambivalent about her and who frequently told her he did not love her.

The peeping occurred when Ruth began to watch (and look for) her boyfriend giving more affection to his daughter. She secretly feasted with her eyes on the sight of "more love" going to the young girl.

The more that Ruth saw the daughter get affection, the more she herself indulged in the feeling of not having it. Then she covered up her attachment by feeling resentful toward the daughter. In this way, she became convinced that her poor relationship with the daughter was the "problem," rather than seeing her own underlying attachment to feeling unloved, and the peeping that was her means to indulge in it.

When it comes to feeling bad, it's hard to beat depression. Most depressions are consequences of an unconscious willingness to indulge in variations of refusal, deprival, control, criticism, and rejection.

So the suffering of a depression can result from an emotional overreaction to some event or situation. For instance, a man became depressed for days because he was insulted by his girlfriend. The suffering he endured with his depression far outweighed the hurt administered by his girlfriend's momentary lapse of sensitivity. The man became depressed not because of the insult in itself, but because of how he reacted to the insult. In other words, he became trapped in his own negative reaction to what was said. He was caught in his indulgence in feeling put down, slighted, seen as unimportant. His attachments to these feelings were the roots of his depression and his low self-esteem.

One woman told me she became depressed after her doctor addressed her in his waiting room by a wrong name, calling her Susan instead of Jane. Anyone can make a mistake such as this. However, this woman had a hard time appreciating her own value, and she used this incident as an opportunity to indulge in feeling less than and unworthy.

Remarkably, a depression can serve as an unconscious defense against the secret attachment to feeling devalued. "I am not looking for this feeling of being put down or devalued," the defense contends. "Look how depressed I am that it is happening to me." Sometimes the inner conscience becomes so severe in its reproaches and condemnations that the task of neutralizing it feels overwhelming. This produces an inner hopelessness that manifests as depression.

Most people can free themselves from their depression when they identify how they are misperceiving key situations in their lives, as they discover and understand the negative feelings they are invested in.

Seeing into Shyness

The shy person is a true flasher. Inwardly, he flashes scenes and visualizations in which he is somehow being defeated, laughed at, or humiliated. His greatest fear is the occurrence of such an experience. His anticipation at being ridiculed paralyzes any positive regard for himself and his life.

Yet, in lieu of the real thing, he produces conscious or subliminal visualizations to this effect—scenes rich with the feeling and sight of his humiliation. He alternates these with scenes in which he is triumphantly humiliating someone else.

As I have said, the first step to gaining control of the emotional imagination is to begin to see and understand your secret attachments to negative emotions that are carried forward from your past. Then you will see that you are producing unpleasant visualizations for the purpose of *feeding* those secret attachments or else *defending* against them. For shy people, the most common attachments are to feeling inadequate, less than, seen as bad, criticized, helpless, and unworthy.

The issues that plague shy and self-conscious individuals can be worked on in group therapy. For example, individuals take turns sitting on a swivel chair in the middle of the room. The rest of the group sits or stands in a circle around the individual. No words are spoken. The person in the middle slowly swivels, making eye contact for ten seconds or so with each member of the group.

He is encouraged to be in touch with his emotional reactions and to try to see how he is projecting certain thoughts or expectations onto the individuals he is looking at. Afterwards, he describes his experience to the group.

A similar procedure is to have each individual take a turn standing in front of the group, as if he were about to give a speech. No words are spoken. He simply looks around at the others, while monitoring his own internal reactions. Still standing in front of the group, he can answer questions put to him by the group leader, i.e. "What are you feeling right now? Is there any tension in your body? If so, where? At what or at who do your eyes want to look? Are there people present who make you feel more comfortable or some who make you feel anxious? Who are they? What would you say it is about them that accounts for your feelings?"

A shy person has a dearth of exhibitionistic self-assertion. The shy person cannot distinguish between appropriate exhibitionism and negative exhibitionism. "I don't want to exhibit and make a fool of myself," he would say of an opportunity to be impressive to others. To show feelings, to let go, to be spontaneous and expressive, is felt to be bad.

Shyness is a frequent reaction when a little boy or girl sees something forbidden. Perhaps it is Mom and Dad naked on their bed. Every child is inclined to link anything to do with sex as forbidden. Now, because of the child's substantial self-centeredness, he feels that being self-expressive (exhibitionistic) in any way will draw attention to himself and somehow reveal what he "should not" have been looking at.

The forbidden something does not have to be sexual. The

peeping inhibition can be experienced when the youngster is exposed to violence, anger, hate, and other abuses and inappropriate behaviors, as the following example illustrates.

A shy client in her mid-twenties had been aware as an adolescent that her parents were using drugs behind their locked bedroom door. "I remember," she said, "I was so afraid of what I knew that on those days I couldn't even ask for a glass of water."

Since the forbidden sight is experienced with such fascination and emotional intensity, it feels to the child that he cannot open his mouth without giving evidence to what he has seen. It feels that he is a walking advertisement for the knowledge of what he has seen, and in his self-centeredness he imagines that what he is thinking and feeling must also be the focus of everyone else's thoughts and feelings.

In order to "prove" that he does not want to exhibit what was seen, and elicit disapproval or punishment, he is silent. The irony is that shy people *do* exhibit negatively because their shyness becomes conspicuous.

Problems of the emotional imagination plagued Jason, a 32-year-old bachelor who came to see me with problems of anger, depression, and acute shyness. He said he was on an emotional roller-coaster, never smiled, and had "been dealt a bad deck." He was not working, his parents paid for his therapy, and he was trying to get a disability pension because of indications of a debilitating disease.

His alcoholic father had been physically abusive toward Jason from the time he was two or three, beating him with a belt and flying into rages over Jason's alleged misbehavior. Jason remembered how shamed he had felt when, stripped along with his younger brother and made to stand against a wall, both were whipped by the father in front of other family members. Jason had ongoing dreams in which violent men came after him, trying to kill him. His mother, meanwhile, was extremely codependent, always making excuses for her husband and defending his behavior.

"I remember always trying to get away from that belt," Jason said. "I don't know why all those beatings were so necessary." Like other victims of child abuse, he had the tendency to defend the perpetrator, saying that his father never beat him unless he had done something bad. Being bad, Jason had to admit, was often nothing more than making noise.

"I will always remember the look my father would give me, especially when he had been drinking," Jason said. "It was hatred, pure hatred, I saw, like he wanted to kill me." He shook his head sadly, adding, "I can picture his face vividly, his disgust for me, especially in the eyes."

As an adult, Jason was living out two messages from his father: "Don't make noise" and "Don't expect anything good to come your way." Jason could barely talk to people, and he lived at home because he had no money to support himself.

Jason's peeping involved looking unconsciously into the faces of people for hateful or disgusted expressions directed back at him. His facial expressions, ranging from a scowl to neutral, constituted negative exhibitionism. Rarely did a thin smile crease his lips.

"I have tended to believe my face is mostly expressionless," he said, "but now I see that often I look quite sad or angry. I've always felt a smile is to be used only when you really like someone."

By looking morose or grim, he helped to ensure that few people would be willing to look back at him with warmth or friendliness. People who were themselves concerned about getting affection or recognition from others would reflect back to Jason whatever they saw on his face. Usually Jason saw what he expected, even from perfect strangers—coldness, indifference, even dislike.

One day in a session, Jason displayed an interesting defense against his attachment to feeling unloved. He had been sitting in the kitchen with his mother that morning, reading the obituary column in the newspaper. She had been talking to him as he read, and he had begun to feel guilty that he was not paying enough attention to her.

Suddenly in the session he began to cry. "I think about her dying," he sobbed. "I have thought about her dying since I was a kid, when I had a nightmare that she had died. I should be there to listen to her now. My mother is my best friend and I won't have her one day when she's gone." His mother, however, was in excellent health. He admitted, "She'll probably live another twenty years."

From childhood, he had frequently imagined his mother laid out in a coffin at the funeral home. The time spent conjuring up images of her death, as well as his tears that afternoon in the session, had little to do with genuine love for her. Rather, Jason was feeling a kind of pseudo-love, produced to bolster this defense against his attachment to feeling unloved: "Look how much I love my mother. This is how I wanted to be treated by her and by my father. If only they had cried for me and treated me with this much love."

As I helped him understand this defense, he admitted he had no concept that it was unusual for a grown man to be so preoccupied with his mother. Like all shy people, Jason had a very hard time establishing a mature, intimate relationship with a sexual partner. He said he liked women but they never stayed around for long. That was not surprising since he was attached to feeling unloved and therefore a "creator" of that experience of life.

Another shy client had difficulty remembering the names of others. She was so self-conscious and so self-absorbed that she didn't really see others, or care about others, as much as she was emotionally preoccupied with how others saw her. She was unable to appreciate others for their own sake. She saw them mainly as judges or critics of her or, when she was comfortable with them, as supporters of her.

A lot of shy people hate themselves. One man told me, "I hate that part of me (shyness) that keeps me from being the person I should be."

I told him, "Hating your shyness is fighting within yourself. It's more productive to understand that your shyness is a way you compensate for your conviction that you will be humiliated or ridiculed by others. The real problem behind your shyness is your unconscious interest in feeling disapproved of or condemned."

Often shy people have the impression they are always doing something wrong. Gerald, a business administrator, had this tendency. He had recently moved into his own private office at work. The office door had a foot-square glass window and Gerald decided to hang a curtain on the inside of the door. There were no regulations about curtains in the windows, so his decision was appropriate.

The next day, however, when Gerald's curtain was closed, a colleague knocked, entered his office, and said teasingly, "Why Jerry, you have hung a curtain over your window and we can't see you. What are you up to now?"

Gerald blushed, sputtered some vague explanation, and immediately felt he had been caught doing something bad. In that moment, he was feeling peeped at, judged, and seen doing it wrong. His thought was, "Oh my, I did it wrong again!" This was the claim-to-power defense ("I cause them to criticize or disapprove of me by messing up somehow.") The defense covered up his secret attachment to being looked at critically and to feeling the disapproval of others.

When he smiled, he was not necessarily happy. He had a frozen smile which he used to defend himself against his attachment to criticism. He fended off disapproval and criticism in his role as a placid people-pleaser. But he had begun to experience tightness in his jaws, especially on rising in the morning. At night, the tension stayed in his face, and he was aware that he ground his teeth while asleep. A few times his jaws had locked. His facial muscles had grown very weary maintaining his persona, this false smile he presented to the world.

Finally, shy people have a difficult time with communication. When their partners want to discuss something intimate, they feel threatened. That is because they are always ready to experience again the feeling of being blamed, disapproved of, criticized, or shamed. Intimacy in relationships requires the expression of one another's fears and feelings. But a shy person feels he will be criticized or rejected for exposing himself, for being himself, and so he holds himself back. If this person can begin to open up and express himself to those he loves, he can make great strides in becoming more confident and self-assured.

Number One Illusion

One of the primary causes of emotional problems and unhappiness is self-centeredness. Self-centeredness is both a cause and an effect of low self-esteem.

The problem of self-centeredness is a hangover from infancy, and it means you are still holding onto the childhood illusion that you are at the center of things and that things are supposed to be the way you think or feel they ought to be. It means responding emotionally as if everyone's focus is on you.

Put another way, self-centeredness is the feeling that the world and others center around you. Even though you know intellectually that this is not logical or realistic, you may still be very self-centered for emotional reasons.

The more you are self-centered, the more you have low self-esteem. The lower your self-esteem, the more likely you are self-centered.

The person with low self-esteem is an emotional pauper caught within his self-imposed square foot of standing in the world. He looks out upon the world from this perspective of his own worthlessness, a point-of-view which binds him to self-centeredness and to his own pain like a martyr to the stake.

Self-centeredness, which originates at birth, may be humanity's number one illusion. It is so powerful in the oral stage that it is called egocentricity or infantile megalomania. This mentality lingers in varying degrees in the adult psyche.

The problem can be seen in history. Back in the Middle Ages, people hated the discovery that the earth was not at the center of the universe; that felt so offensive to the wish to be at the center. People hated it when Charles Darwin discovered evolution; that meant they were not custom-made in the image of God. People hated it when Sigmund Freud discovered the unconscious; that meant they were not at the center of self-control but reacting to the dynamics of drives, impulses, and conditioning beyond their awareness.

All of us tend to approach our lives from a self-centered perspective. We are certainly being self-centered when we talk about ourselves a lot, when we feel the desire to be at the center of attention, when we insist on getting our way, when we're not interested in other people's thoughts or feelings, and when we're easily insulted and take things personally.

Each of us also reacts from self-centeredness when we are upset that someone gets a larger raise or a promotion, or when we protest that our food is not cooked exactly right. It is from a self-centered perspective that we would want to control our kids to be like us, become anxious when others question our beliefs, or worry about not having enough wealth when we are already prosperous. We are being especially self-centered when we focus time and consideration on what others may think of us.

Here's an example of everyday self-centeredness. A husband gets mad at his wife for coming home an hour late and forgetting to get coffee at the store. He is not interested in his wife's story or explanation. He is emotionally preoccupied with the feeling, "What about me!" This focus on his own deprivation or neglect is a childish reaction that causes emotional distress.

From self-centeredness, a big concern becomes the maintenance of your self-importance (a corollary of self-centeredness). You are triggered or emotionally agitated when others appear to ignore you, to look down on you, or to refuse you. So we spend much of our time being offended by someone or something.

This self-importance also becomes a compensation for underlying feelings of insecurity. With this problem, you unconsciously look for people to treat you with disrespect, and you are at the mercy of any fool or nincompoop who may decide, for his own unconscious reasons, he does not like you.

If someone does not like you, or if he withholds from you, your self-importance will produce a negative reaction such as anger, the desire for revenge, or a critical attitude toward him. It feels as if he is your enemy. But he is only the enemy of your self-importance.

You will even suffer if, in your mind, someone does not like you enough. Or if someone does not give you enough.

In self-centeredness, we see the world from the me-mine-more mentality of the oral stage. We see through a veil of prejudices, identifications, roles, beliefs, fears, and desires. We see the world subjectively, in terms of our own relationship to it. These are the veils of "psycho-myopia," producing illusions, distortions, and misunderstandings.

Your emotional preoccupation is, "How is the world treating me right now? How am I being let down, disappointed, not given to? Who is mean or unfair to me, and how am I being victimized?" Everything we see is in terms of how it affects us. It is easy to be bored, confused, frustrated, or angry when we see the world from this mentality.

In contrast, the person with more self-esteem sees the world without judgment and regret, without feelings of being gypped or deprived or victimized. He sees the world with more appreciation and wonder. He looks for beauty or for what is amusing or pleasurable. He also sees more clearly what has to be done and what he is able to do for the benefit of himself and others.

Greed is a direct consequence of self-centeredness and self-importance. Greed is entirely focused around me, mine, more. More specifically, greed is an expression of the fear of (and attachment to) deprivation, missing out, refusal, or loss.

An extreme form of self-centeredness is self-absorption. Addictive and compulsive personalities are self-absorbed because their substantial underlying emotional problems keep them bound in constant inner conflict. An important element in the cure or recovery of these people involves growing awareness of the degree of their self-absorption.

Another variation on self-centeredness is self-pity. This occurs specifically when a person is indulging or wallowing in the feeling of being a victim. I had a client who felt sorry for himself because, as he saw it, he was born in the wrong century for adventure and romance. It was to his great regret he missed out wearing a Confederate uniform and fighting against the North in the Civil War.

A very self-centered person, who often appears normal to people, is the charming psychopath. The word *psychopath* is frequently mistaken for the psychotic sociopath. The former is not necessarily psychotic or violent as the sociopath is. Rather, the psychopath is extremely self-centered and narcissistic.

Such types are often intelligent, articulate, and assertive. To the naive observer they may appear quite healthy. In fact, they often appear to be the embodiment of self-esteem. However, they are chronic liars who, in fact, may believe their own lies because they are too heavily defended to begin to fathom the degree of their distorted perceptions.

Frequently, psychopaths make good con-artists because

they are so convincing. Naive individuals often find themselves attracted to a psychopath because he can look them in
the eye and make them feel like very important persons. The
average person has his share of insecurities and consequently
likes the feeling of being seen as important. Hence, he likes
anyone who appears to see him in this light.

I mention psychopaths here at some length because they
are the epitome of the self-important mentality. They often
rise to the top of hierarchies in corporations, institutions,
and politics because people cannot see through them, are
mesmerized by them, and will not stand up to their intimi-
dating manner.

Some low self-esteem people concede power to a psychopathic personality because, unconsciously, they are aligned
with the feeling of being controlled, dominated, and directed
by someone who "knows," someone with apparent authority,
a "father figure" who regresses them into their childhood
experiences of passivity.

The psychopath is so much consumed by his own self-
importance that he is insensitive to the feelings or points-of-
view of others. He is aware of the next person only as an image in his mind, and his reactions are to the image rather than
the real person. He is even an image to himself. All his energy
is focused on enhancing or protecting his self-image. So his
strategy is to win people over through charm and apparent
openness, to have them buy into his self-image.

This personality represents an unconscious attempt to restore the lesion in self-esteem caused by the blows to megalomania sustained in his early childhood. "It is not true I
want to feel refused or rejected or unloved," says his defense.
"Look at all the attention I give to myself."

The psychopath has a full expression of childish egocentrism
unhampered by accommodations to others or to reality. He has
an extreme degree of low self-esteem or he would not have to

go to such lengths to prove himself to others. He represents the antithesis of humility and is what we all would have become if we had not made appropriate compromises within ourselves to recognize and integrate reality.

The criminal mind (often psychopathic) represents another extreme form of self-centeredness and another variation on oral conflicts. The criminal sees the world almost like a baby. He is full of infantile fury, bent on revenge for alleged injustices he felt he suffered from earliest childhood. Unconsciously, he is extremely passive, feeling hopeless in impressing his rage upon the offenders of his megalomania (first mother, then society). Consequently, he resorts to primitive aggression to cover this deep passivity and to "succeed" in calling attention to the enormity of his gripes. Unconsciously, he is attached to being caught, subjugated, and punished, as his foolish "slip-ups" attest.

In summary, we are all self-centered to some degree. Self-centeredness in the adult represents the persistence of the child's emotional experiences and perceptions, reflects how those emotional memories continue to determine our behaviors and feelings, and explains why we react childishly in many of the emotional events of our lives.

Part II

Origins and Examples

Passivity And Shame

European child-raising instruction manuals of 100 years ago advised parents to break a child's will and independent spirit at an early age. Absolute submission, obedience, and loyalty were expected of children. It was understood that adults were never wrong or mistaken, and that it was appropriate to condemn a child if necessary and impart to him the feeling that he was guilty and bad.

Verbal and physical abuse were considered acceptable to achieve these aims. In fact, the rise of fascism in Europe is attributed to the family model where Dad was dictator, Mom was Dad's backup (the Gestapo), and children were passive victims and followers.

Thankfully, these manuals are no longer in print. But a subtle form of inappropriate child-raising persists in what can be called *The Great Law*. This law is held in force by the negative repetition compulsion, whereby parents repeat with their kids the corruption or inappropriate behavior that they were passively required to endure at the hands of their own parents. This problem passes down from generation to generation, and only the right education can break the cycle.

Under *The Great Law,* children enter an unconscious agreement or silent pact with their parents. The children then grow up being what others expect of them or believing what others tell them about themselves, rather than discovering their own intrinsic value and purpose.

It feels to the child that his or her withholding of contrary feelings and perceptions is taken as love by the parents. One client had a mother who had been obsessed about keeping her house immaculately clean. The mother convinced him and his sisters to "buy into" her perceptions, to aid her in a daily scourge of household dirt. She claimed that through such sacrifice they proved their love for her. The children surrendered to her insistence and her flawed perceptions and grew up to be obsessive-compulsive personality types.

Perhaps a child has been scorned or humiliated for his own self-expression. At age three, a client of mine had been stripped and then whipped by his father for being "mouthy" at the dinner table.

The child understands that truth in the family setting is only what the parents, in their narcissism, are willing to hear and consider. If the child feels shamed for what he feels and perceives, he retreats into silence and perhaps into shyness. He keeps quiet, obeys, and then discounts his own perceptions. He fails to develop his own unique sense of self, and soon the family dysfunction is accepted as "normal."

The child perceives that his feelings and beliefs do not have any value to the parents. Often this is reality—the parent is interested only in his own point of view and in getting the child to validate that point of view. A client had recently driven home from a movie with her mother and father. Every time my client tried to express her views of the film, her father cut her off with his own comments. "Sad to say," she said later, "but he is only interested in the sound of his own voice. He does not have the ability to actually listen with interest to what someone else is saying. He hasn't changed one bit in thirty years."

To the child, it feels as if the parents are not interested in him. He grows up feeling that he is not seen as having any value in his own right, and he feels shame for being so unworthy. He lacks discernment as an adult and believes the most blatant lies. Because he does not trust his perceptions, he goes along with the prevailing views or relies on the interpretations of others. He believes he is helpless and powerless with others, which is the way he felt as a child.

He or she will resist truth and insight because it is "bad," as it was in childhood. As an adult, he identifies with his parents who lied about themselves. Like Mom and Dad, he finds it easy to pretend that nothing is wrong. He only sees what he wants to believe. As an adult, he does not take the risks needed to advance himself, thereby maintaining his sense of boredom and failure. Yet, he insists that his lack of success is always someone else's fault.

Government and corporations have this tendency too—expecting submission to their will. Some corporations expect complete loyalty from employees, including tacit approval if not participation in any corruptions. In some of its covert operations, the government behaves like neurotic parents: it is expected you will not ask embarrassing questions and information is kept from you, allegedly "for your own good." If you do not approve, you are bad, disloyal. In any run-in with the government, the fear we feel is the same as a kid's in challenging the beliefs and perceptions of his parents.

However, it is very important to understand that inappropriate child-raising *is not the only cause of passivity and shame.* A later chapter, "Forbidden Sights," explains how children can feel shame for wanting so desperately to see certain sights, particularly of a sexual nature, which they feel are forbidden. There is another important consideration. When a child is being reprimanded for minor infractions (making noise, not taking out the garbage, etc.), he is usually not able to distinguish between himself and his behavior. His egocentricity or extreme self-centeredness makes it difficult for him to distinguish himself, his own essence, from his actions. It is easy for him to feel that if his actions are being criticized or condemned, he is being condemned as a person.

Of course, as adults we may continue to have this problem, which explains why we become so defensive or react so emotionally when our behaviors are challenged.

A parent can tell his child, "I am reprimanding your behavior, not you as a person. I love you but I am not happy with your behavior." This may help the child to understand, but sometimes a child is so intent on taking things the wrong way that he will not be impressed by what you say in this respect. Some kids handle the process of their socialization better than others. Many good parents have a child who is completely unreasonable and unmanageable and who is determined to feel deprived, inadequate, controlled, criticized, or rejected. This is because the child's unconscious attachments to these feelings are powerful, despite his best conscious efforts to behave appropriately.

If shame is a familiar feeling for you, insight will help you the most. (Shame is a result of feeling condemned as a person, worthless in your very essence or, as the rock lyrics put it, "bad to the bone.") Regardless of the behavior of your parents in contributing to your emotional predicament, you are now stuck with an attachment to feeling condemned. Blaming your parents, even if they were ignorant and cruel, only strengthens your sense of being a victim. You need to deal with the lingering attachment to feeling condemned that makes you feel bad about yourself. Attachments can be worked out and neutralized once you see how readily you are lured back into experiences of those old negative feelings.

Perfect parents don't exist. Blaming decent parents for not being perfect and for allegedly causing shame in their children is like blaming God for a rainy day.

I have seen many clients who quickly feel wrong about themselves when I begin to analyze them. They feel condemned because they take the analysis as criticism, disapproval, and an indication of their unworthiness. Even those who had decent and loving parents may be quick to use any opportunity or "evidence" to feel wrong about themselves.

They may even interpret reality from these extremes: "If the therapist (onto whom they transfer Dad or Mom) is right, then I am wrong." Sometimes they sacrifice all redeeming qualities in themselves for the sake of the other person and give themselves over to the control and authority of the other person. They feel so wrong in themselves as to feel annihilated, that they don't exist emotionally, and the other person (originally mother or father) becomes the adjudicator of who they are and what they are worth.

Different religions also use shame and guilt to influence and control people. People may allow a religion to judge their value or lack of value. Shame is implied in the message that we are no-good sinners barely worthy of redemption. Individuals with enduring experiences of shame from their childhoods will be among the leaders of these types of religions as well as among the passive followers. Many people have been quick to identify and label "a scarlet woman" because they secretly identify with her and thereby experience indirectly the feeling from their own past of being shamed.

Parents often use shame to control a child and make him conform. Sometimes shame is used against the child in toilet training and other experiences of early socialization, and often this child grows up to be angry, shy, or withdrawn with no memories of those experiences to help him understand his emotions. Despite not having conscious memories, the experience of repeatedly having been shamed as a child makes the adult feel he will be shamed again if he comes out of his shyness, out of hiding. So his lack of emotional openness and vulnerability is a block to intimacy with others and inhibits other pleasures.

The use of shame in child-raising passes on from generation to generation because each new set of parents is conditioned to have their children experience what they themselves passively endured. When an attachment to shame is not worked out, the parents are compelled to create situations with their own children in which they will identify unconsciously with the shame that their children are experiencing.

Shame is a major problem for many addictive personalities. I have seen the problem most pronounced in alcoholics and bulimics. Women who binge and purge will then follow up that experience by tormenting themselves with severe self-condemnation. The consequence is to feel profound shame.

Men experience the feeling just as much through other addictions and compulsions, as well as through their performance and standing in the world. Compulsive gamblers, for example, likely spend more time enveloped in shame than they do at the race track.

In my approach to treatment, I help these individuals understand that shame is experienced because they "buy into" the feeling of being condemned. A person feels shame to the degree that he believes he deserves to be punished for allegedly doing something wrong or bad (or for being wrong or bad). A five-year-old sees her father standing naked in his bedroom. Her mother appears and says disapprovingly, "What are *you* looking at!" The girl retreats in shame, convinced she was bad for the "crime" of peeping. But the real "crime" behind the shame, however, is her attachment to being exposed and seen negatively by her mother. The feeling of shame is her unconscious identification with how she imagines her father feels in being seen naked.

The following is what I call *The Emotional Structure of Low Self-Esteem*. The structure consists of three layers. Imagine a three-layer wedding cake, with the top layer representing what we are aware of about ourselves, while the bottom two layers represent emotional dynamics and reactions in the unconscious mind.

At the top layer (conscious), the low self-esteem individual spends a lot of time worrying about what others think of him. He may be full of shame and sometimes seized with fear and panic about the possibility of others discovering that he is "no good" and a "fake." He may become a people-pleaser as he tries to prove how valuable he is or how well he is liked by others. Or he may act out in self-defeating or anti-social behaviors and thereby exhibit, for all to see, his emotional conviction that he is no good.

At different times, he is plagued with doubt about himself. He sometimes imagines himself being refused or controlled or rejected by others. Often he feels like he doesn't belong, and he wonders if he's good enough. He feels like a failure, like a victim. He may feel helpless to do anything to improve his circumstances, and sometimes he is tempted to give up on himself.

At the next layer, the middle layer, his mental and emotional operations are sometimes conscious, but most often unconscious. Here the individual claims power by believing that he causes others to see him as not having any value. His claims to power involve the "admission" of certain "crimes" such as, I'm bad, or lazy, or irresponsible, not good enough, inadequate, stupid, greedy, selfish, ugly, powerless, and so on.

His defense may go like this: "I, through my own negligence or stupidity, cause them to devalue me and discredit me." Now the person beats up on himself for these alleged crimes. He buys into the negative inner voices scolding him for these alleged crimes as he punishes himself with guilt and shame. This distracts attention from (defends against) the real underlying issue.

That underlying issue is at the roots of low self-esteem. Here we get to the third or bottom layer (unconscious), where it is our secret attachments that keep us mired in negativity and shame. These attachments are well defended; we are not supposed to know about them. All of our defenses are designed to keep us from being aware of our attachments. These attachments include the unconscious willingness to be seen by parents, and later by others, as being inadequate, defective, perhaps having no value, and to feel deprived, refused, controlled, rejected, and criticized.

Deep down, these are the feelings you keep coming back to like a dog to his dirty old bone: "I am nothing to them. I have no value as a person in my own right. I am helpless as they look at me and discredit me, along with my feelings and opinions. I am 'into' being seen by others as inferior and a failure. I look to be accused of wrongdoing and caught doing something bad. I 'take a hit' off the feeling of being shamed and humiliated by others."

The sad truth is that you are not only entangled in those feelings, you are willing to indulge in them and you are resistant to letting go of them. This is how we unconsciously maintain our low self-esteem. For some, it feels easier to live in ignorance and denial rather than to see this, even if the denial means they must also live in pain, guilt, and shame. But ignorance is *not* bliss. Whoever said otherwise was concocting another self-defeating defense.

Parental Messages

Separate from *The Great Law* is another important set of childhood circumstances that affect our self-esteem. These are *parental messages,* and they consist of actual, implied, or misunderstood statements from parents concerning their impressions of us as children and their expectations for us.

Parental messages can have a negative or a positive bias, yet even what appear on the surface to be positive messages can be interpreted by a child in a negative manner.

Alice, a 35-year-old accountant, was an addictive personality with substantial emotional problems. She recalled that her father had urged her from the time she was an adolescent to get a Ph.D., to be a teacher, to become accomplished, and to meet important people. He frequently expressed positive goals for her and appeared to imagine a bright future.

At the same time, however, it felt to Alice that he only gave lip-service to the idea of her independence, and that he really wanted her to be tied to him emotionally and live for him rather than have a life of her own. In other words, Alice could be successful and independent but not without him as a dominant force in her life.

She felt this way not because of direct statements from him to this effect but from his attitude and behavior toward her which revealed his egotistical belief that the lives of all family members revolved around him. For instance, Alice was expected to confirm his decisions and accept his help in all matters. It was expected she would want to be involved in her parents' home life even as an adult.

Alice acquired the following feelings about herself based on her father's attitude and behavior toward her: "I'm really bad; he feels sad for me; I am vulnerable, fragile, and insecure; I am always ready to fail and will need to be rescued; I am unable to make good decisions for myself."

Like her mother, Alice was intimidated by him and never did stand up to him before she left home as an adult. She said it would have felt wrong to say no to him or to disagree with him. "I just knew he would manipulate my mind or twist my words around to convince me to accept his point of view. It felt I would have no chance against him."

Even with good parents, children will tend to believe on an emotional level what is said or implied about them that is negative. Children will buy into these negative messages or implications to the core of their being, and these messages about themselves will haunt them and determine how they feel about themselves when they are adults.

Remember, we looked up to our parents as if they were gods. From that perspective, it felt as if they looked down on us. We didn't know why they apparently devalued us or looked down on us. So we believed we caused it to happen. We made a *claim-to-power* defense (described in *The Emotional Structure of Low Self-Esteem* in the previous chapter). In our self-centeredness, we made the claim that we were responsible for being devalued by our parents. It must be something we did, or something about us, that was wrong or bad. We will say the problem is that we're not smart enough, not pretty enough, or not worthy, or too fat, too skinny, too weak, too mean, too sinful, too lazy, whatever. Now, unfortunately, we will feel bad about ourselves for this alleged wrongdoing. Shame, guilt, doubt, anxiety, fear, sadness, and depression are common ways we feel bad about ourselves.

A parent needs to know that what he says to his child that is demeaning or derogatory represents how he feels about himself. That means the weakness you see and dislike in your child is the weakness you are refusing to see in yourself. For instance, a father is describing how little he values himself when he says to his son, "Who do you think you are!" Insecurities or fears that you try to hide or ignore in yourself are passed along subliminally to your children, and your children become conditioned to pass those feelings on to their own children.

The self-esteem of parents directly affects children. Feelings of being defective or flawed or worthless can simply be passed on from parents to children, from generation to generation. When parents don't value themselves, they'll have trouble valuing their children. They won't take their children seriously nor really listen to them. Subliminally, a child picks up from his parents how they feel about themselves—and that will be how he feels about himself.

The message may be, "No one cares what you think," or "Greatness is beyond your reach," or "Just consider yourself lucky to get by."

James, another client, remembered how blatantly his mother had transferred her insecurities onto him. "Mother really experienced her insecurities after talking on the phone with her brother or sister, both of whom she felt inferior to," he said. "They spent most of the conversation time talking about how well their kids were doing academically and socially. After those talks, Mom would come out into the living room and say to us in an anxious voice, 'You should hear how well your cousins are doing. Shouldn't you kids be making more friends. Shouldn't you be doing better in school.'

"It didn't matter that we were okay, and doing fine," James continued. "She had to imply that we weren't good enough. And I could tell in her voice how strongly she felt that we were inflicted with some fatal flaws and weren't really going to amount to much. The feeling is still there. This is what I'm working on."

His success had been motivated by low self-esteem. James set out to prove in the eyes of his mother and others that he was not inadequate or worthless, as he felt himself to be. Unfortunately, desperation marked his pursuit of success, and it was often achieved at the expense of others or in a compulsive manner that left no room for fun or pleasure. Until he began to work on his psychology, his inner sense of worthlessness had remained.

The single most common inner message that torments us is, "I'm not good enough." As children, it was our conviction that somehow we didn't live up to our parents' expectations. We believed that when they were raising us, they weren't guiding and helping us so much as they were (in our eyes) refusing us, depriving us, controlling us, criticizing us, and taking us for granted. We took on these negative feelings and believed our parents felt this way about us because of alleged flaws or deficiencies within us. The result was to feel bad or ashamed of ourselves for these alleged shortcomings and inadequacies.

A child can also feel insecure when he gets excessive praise from parents. When a parent overexaggerates a child's accomplishments, the child may feel that who he is as a person in his own right is not enough—that he has to be exceptional just to be okay. He also has no room for mistakes, and he can feel that to fail is to be seen as having no value.

Whatever is harsh and unreasonable in a parent's attitude

and behavior toward his child is incorporated into the child's own inner conscience where the harshness is exaggerated to become inner voices of self-doubt, self-reproach, and self-condemnation. Here are some of the inner messages my clients have directed at themselves: "What is wrong with you—you are always messing up! You should have known better! This is not going to work out—you never do anything right. You are no good—and everyone knows you are worthless." And my favorite is, "Once again you have gone and behaved like an idiot!" (I say more about this problem in a later chapter, "Frankenstein Is Here").

Often we want to blame our problems on other people. We become convinced they prevent us from doing what we want (just like our parents did). So we struggle to be free of their expectations and demands, unaware that we are really fighting within ourselves. As long as you believe that your conflicts or problems are with someone outside of yourself, you can do little but complain and feel sorry for yourself. When you realize that these conflicts originate within you, then you can take responsibility for your own difficulties and stop blaming the world for the emotional problems that are really your own.

However, many people do blame themselves, but for the wrong reasons. I emphasize again, you must see *correctly* your own involvement (make conscious what was unconscious) in order to overcome the elements that hold you back, maintain your unhappiness, and promote self-defeat.

Once you do, you tap into the power within yourself to make the creative changes you want, enabling you to feel your autonomy and independence. Remember, it is your willingness to be responsible for whatever negative emotions you are experiencing that brings you a sense of power and capability.

The most important consideration for you now is discovering the degree to which you continue to hold onto the negative messages that you experienced in your family of origin. Whether your parents made life difficult for you or not, a part of you remains attached to old negative feelings of low self-worth.

To get a deeper sense of how you felt growing up in your family, ask yourself the following questions: What did Mom and Dad say they wanted me to be? How did Mom and Dad really feel about me? What did they think of my personality? If I asserted my true feelings, how would they have reacted? How did I feel emotionally, and why? What messages did they give me about my competence and my ability to make my own decisions? Was I expected to accept their views and beliefs, or encouraged to appreciate my independent perspective?

Now look at your entire life. Make a connection between your perceptions of your parents' expectations and messages about you, and what you feel has happened to you, or what you have become. Are you a conformist or a rebel? Try to see how you might have lived out what your parents expected of you, and whether you are still intent on getting their approval. Or perhaps you have been rebelling against what your parents expected of you, a reaction that may also be self-defeating.

Boyhood Dreams

My boyhood dream was to reach a time and place where I could feel good about myself. The sooner the better because from ages twelve to sixteen I was mired in existential misery.

At twelve I developed a kind of "psycho-myopia" that required me to wear glasses for near-sightedness. I did not want to see something in the family dynamic. I did not want to see the degree to which my parents were not conscious of me as a value in my own right, as I saw them spinning around in their own self-absorption.

I followed in their footsteps, into the darkness of my own self-absorption. From there I saw a world indifferent and even hostile to my existence.

Of course, my parents looked my way at times with interest in me as a person. But it felt as if they did not really see me. Once when I was in my twenties, I challenged my mother about her method of making French toast, claiming she did not soak the bread long enough in the batter (I suppose I was giving her a taste of the know-it-all attitude she had dished out to me). She looked at me as if for the first time, and in that moment I felt she really took notice of me as a person with my own independent perspective.

Growing up at home, I became convinced by the time I was seven or eight that my feelings, my viewpoints, and my pain did not matter to them. In my family, it felt as if we were not supposed to have emotional problems, nor even expressions of our emotional nature. Such expression meant you were weak and bad. Dad and Mom never actually said that. It was just understood. To be vulnerable or weak invited scorn and humiliation.

My parents did take some interest in my endeavors—projects, grades, art, reading. But from my father, I often felt what I did or said was never good enough. I felt a lot of scorn and indifference from him, which is what he had felt from his father. And from my mother I felt that I could not be myself. I had to be molded to her mentality. She only found me acceptable when I saw things or did things her way. I had to be what she and Dad expected of me—somehow to be perfect and grow up and be an engineer or medical doctor.

My first boyhood dream was to escape to manhood and live far away from home. My second dream was to become a great champion of the links. The pleasure of golf was one salvation in my difficult teenage years. My golf course was a little nine-hole affair, my psychic safety valve on Sisco Island in sub-tundra Quebec, 350 miles north of Montreal.

In late May, snow still lingered in the woods, icy and dirty, refusing to concede the change of seasons. We got to drop the ball without penalty one club-length from the snow; that was how I cheated winter until I moved to Florida.

But on beautiful days in July and August we moved from shot to shot pursuing birdies and eagles like hunters in a dream. By mid-September, cold winds off the lake rolled across the eighth and then the third fairways, stripping the yellow birch and poplar leaves and blowing them into the woods on the left side of the 260-yard fifth hole where I hook-ed and lost more balls than any teenager in Quebec.

My nemisis was my balky visual drive. I blinked or my eyes went dead at that critical moment of clubface impact upon the ball. Even when my head stayed still, the quality of my visual contact was questionable, for self-defeating imaginings from my dark side were peering down the fairway an instant before the ball was hit, so eager to see how well I would *mis-hit* it.

Sometimes I looked up prematurely for what I now know was the secret thrill of seeing the ball going where it was not supposed to.

My self-defeating side followed me onto the golf course to make sure I did not have too much fun. Nervous hands were a problem, but mostly it was that balky visual drive, my emotional imagination.

When the best golfers fail to do well, especially under pressure, this is one of the ways they defeat themselves. Many aspiring players do not reach heights of excellence because of what they do not know about the emotional imagination. Even when the head is still through impact and the eyes are looking at the ball, there are still variations in the quality of visual contact with the ball and in the swing that are determined by the person's unconscious capacity for self-defeat. In his emotional imagination, the self-defeater does not see or imagine himself as a winner or a champion.

The most fun I ever had with my Dad and my Mom was on the golf course. We have played hundreds of time, the three of us. I never felt better than when they oohed and aahed my good shots.

If they could not love me for my own essence, I would settle for the feeling of being admired for my prowess as a golfer. Under these conditions, my inner saboteur took much satisfaction in having me misuse my emotional imagination to flub up with victory in sight (that being the feeling of their enhanced respect for me), and recreate the feeling of failure by duffing my way along the final few fairways.

One problem was that old refrain I had picked up from my father and had incorporated into the core of my being, "You're not supposed to be too good." Other times, whiplashing me in contradictions, he had screamed at me, "I don't want my son to be a bum!"

Those dual messages were killers. One time my parents were full of praise, telling me how clever I was, that I could achieve the highest goals. Other times, and especially on an inner level that I picked up subliminally, they were critical and judgmental, and I was convinced they held me in little regard, despite their words to the contrary.

Yes, that was the message I took to heart: "Mustn't be too good." To be good would make Dad look bad. If I were to shine, he would feel less than. I remember that look of alarm on his face when I was really feeling assertive, expressive, and free. "Don't be too cocky!" he liked to say—sternly.

It can still make me anxious to be seen with respect and admiration. For a long time, being seen as someone smart and strong felt strange, alien, even threatening. Other people have this feeling too. I call it, "Resistance To Being Too Good," and I have deduced five emotional reasons for this resistance in my own situation:

1) If I were too good, others wouldn't like me. My father was never comfortable with the idea I might become "better" than him. Later in his life, he was nervous around me whenever my psychological insights were on display. 2) If I were too good, people would want more from me. There would be more expectations placed on me, and I would be drained or exploited. 3) I might be used for the narcissism of others. They would want to "hang out" with me because that would make them look good. I would feel used, exploited. 4) People would

think that I think too much of myself. "Don't be too cocky!" my father told me at least 100 times. That implied that I was exhibiting, and that was apparently bad. 5) If I were too good, then Mom and Dad were great parents and couldn't be faulted for anything. That would let them off the hook—and I would have to give up my attachment to holding them accountable for my failures.

I'm getting better, mostly because I *see* how I have used this stuff against myself.

So our parents were less than perfect. By the time we are adults, however, our problems are not now caused by our parents or by others but are a result of our own emotional reactions to people, events, or circumstances. We are up against a part of ourselves that is quite willing, even eager, to rush in and feel victimized in some context or other.

The greatest struggle in my life has been to accept who I am. I felt like a shipwrecked sailor clinging to a shroud of hope in an ocean of low self-esteem. Without self-esteem I was half a person, wounded, and in chronic emotional pain. I have discovered that, despite the weaknesses of my parents, my low self-esteem resulted primarily from my misperceptions as a child. I took so personally the attitudes and actions of my parents and sisters toward me.

We can see clearly that self-esteem is influenced by external variables such as the self-esteem of the parents, by the quality of the parents' relationship with their children and each other, by the attitude of the family to the outside world, and by how siblings treat and regard each other.

More difficult to understand are the roles of internal determinants of self-esteem. These determinants have to do with how each individual child assimilates and processes his experiences of being socialized—meaning corrected, guided, reproached, and punished. Why does one child and not another become emotionally convinced of his lack of value when his

parents are too busy for him, when they scold him for misbe-
haviors, when he feels controlled or dominated by them, and
when they don't fulfill his expectations?

To what degree does the child take corrections or criticism
as an indication that he is bad, wrong, or flawed in some way?
If a child has an unkind or alcoholic father who ignores him, to
what degree does the child become convinced that his own
deficiencies or inadequacies somehow cause his father to ignore him?

The modern fad of blaming parents or circumstances for
one's emotional problems represents an easy way out for lots
of people. These people do not want to see (let alone take
responsibility for) the continuation in their present lives of
their own negativity and patterns of self-defeat. They want to
believe that, as children, they were sweet innocents subjected
to bad outside influences and that their parents are responsible through mistreatment, neglect, or ignorance for their
present misery. The more they believe that, the more they will
become mired in low self-esteem, convinced they are the
legitimate victims of the negligence and malice of others.

The adult with low self-esteem carries within himself secret
attachments to being seen as inadequate, less than, bad, unworthy. He then proceeds to find his own self-defeating ways to
act out his emotional convictions. He may also be the most
critical judge of his own value, and often inner voices (an
expression of the self-aggression we all deal with) assail him
with recrimination and reproach for his alleged shortcomings more harshly than anyone else would dare.

Sometimes, we can feel that our culture or society is part of
the problem. Indeed, it is true we are always being judged for
something, whether it is for clothes, homes, bank accounts,
jobs, education, physical features, or baseball-card collections.
But the person with low self-esteem is already expecting Ds
and Fs on the report card of life. His mentality, identity, or

sense of self is preoccupied with being judged as bad and deemed unworthy. Often when he does get praise and recognition, he is uncomfortable with those positive feelings, and he may even belittle his own accomplishments.

I have looked at and worked with my own substantial attachments to being seen as inadequate. One day while working on this book I wrote 2,500 words that I felt were creative and insightful. That same day, however, inner voices were quietly intimating to me that I was secretly entertaining expectations of having my writing judged as inadequate and being rejected. I did not realize this until after a dream I had that night.

In the dream, I was promoted to the rank of general and being sent off to an overseas war zone. Crowds cheered me on my way to the Tampa airport in an open-air limosine for my flight to the Middle East. This is called a dream of refutation. In it I tried to establish a defense (that I want to be cheered and admired) to cover up my attachment to being judged critically. My identification with the general and my thrill in waving to the cheering crowds were intended to "prove" that I really did want acceptance and admiration. Seeing through this defense, and diagnosing this latest flare-up of my attachment to being rejected, was the best possible medicine to keep bad feelings about myself at bay.

Understanding Orality

To understand the emotional imagination and its relationship to low self-esteem, you have to understand the concept of orality. That is because the peeping or voyeuristic instincts of the emotional imagination are a kind of "orality of the eyes."

Orality is a term that describes a child's consciousness during the first eighteen months of life, a time when the child's impressions of the world are based on various illusions such as king-size megalomania and baby fears, as well as rebounding aggression and emotional rages, ambivalence toward the mother-object, frustrating helplessness, and satisfactions and dissatisfactions experienced through the mucous membranes of the mouth.

Our oral history hangs around in the adult psyche, deeply repressed, making all kinds of trouble for unsuspecting adults. Sigmund Freud did not expound much on orality because he was uncovering the mysteries of two later stages of childhood development, the anal stage from eighteen months to three years and especially the genital stage from three years to five years.

However, much has been revealed about orality from the writings of psychoanalyst Edmund Bergler, a medical graduate of the University of Vienna. Bergler wrote almost 300 published articles and twenty-two books on the subject before his death in New York City in 1962. He has been pretty well ignored because people hated to hear or reflect upon what he said, and consequently the world has not been able to assimilate the meaning and significance of what he discovered.

Bergler realized that a primary weakness of human nature is the unconscious tendency to play the role of the victim in some context or other and to be drawn into negative feelings by the unconscious attachments we develop. As mentioned, attachments to negative feelings constitute the unconscious willingness (based on childhood experiences and perceptions) to become entangled in feeling deprival, refusal, loss, control, domination, helplessness, rejection, betrayal, criticism, and so on. The consequences lead us to experience repeatedly a wide range of negative emotions and self-defeating reactions.

Larry's story illustrates oral conflicts as well as problems of low self-esteem. A forty-year-old real-estate agent, he revealed the following information about himself in our first session. He was depressed and crying a lot, feeling sorry for himself, and worried about his finances. A business he owned had failed a year or so earlier, and he was not doing well in the real-estate slump. His wife worked only part-time in order to be with their young son. "I'm feeling like a dead-beat," he said, "and dreadful about not being able to take better care of my family."

His mother had died four months earlier, and he was "devastated." He cried daily over the loss of his mother. He had endured the same kind of feeling for two years following the death of his father several years earlier.

A friend of Larry's had lost his wife and child in a car crash the year before, and Larry was deeply involved emotionally in his friend's tragic loss. Larry also said he spent considerable time brooding about his own son, worrying that his son would grow up without the amenities and advantages of a financially secure family.

"I want everything for him," Larry said. "But I'm afraid for him, that he will grow up being deprived." Then he added, "I admit that I have a crummy attitude about life in general."

Larry's problem involved an unconscious fascination with the prospects of loss, missing out, and being deprived. He suffered more than was necessary following the deaths of his parents. And he was not even grieving for them. Instead, he was feeling sorry for himself as he indulged in his own sense of loss.

He identified with his friend who had lost his wife and child in a car crash, and he slipped into the skin of his friend, vicariously feeling another variation on loss. When he brooded about his son's bleak future, he had found yet another way to accentuate his own affinity for the bleakness of life.

A year earlier Larry's own business had gone into bankruptcy. Financial loss such as this often happens to people with this oral mentality. They use events or situations in their lives to experience some form of loss. For instance, such people are prone to put their money in risky investments hoping for a big return. They are anxious to "prove" how much they want to get in order to cover up their attachment to loss. Yet the conditions they create are such that their risk of loss is greater.

This kind of self-defeat defies common sense—but remember we are dealing with irrational processes. For Larry, his unconscious problem with loss was like having a saboteur as a business partner.

With the feeling of being a "deadbeat," Larry blamed himself for his plight and felt terrible about himself. The individual makes the claim to power ("I cause it to happen") to cover up his passivity, his willingness to indulge in the loss. However, once the individual sees the unconscious dynamics and becomes more deeply aware of them, he can begin to have power over his self-defeating side, and he becomes capable of growth and reform.

Larry's claim that he was a deadbeat covered up his substantial passivity and secret willingness to be entangled in the clutches of his attachment to loss. Making the claim to be a deadbeat produced guilt and shame, and that required him to suffer all the implications of being "a dismal failure." But the root of the problem was his unresolved orality—his attachment to feelings of loss and deprivation.

Involuntarily, Larry used his emotional imagination to feed his oral problem. He often drove through rich neighborhoods lusting after all the luxury he saw. The word *covet* captures the essence of his negative peeping. A person often covets what he cannot have or what is forbidden, his neighbor's wife for instance. It means the person consumes with his eyes that which is beyond his reach or is unavailable, thereby generating a desire, longing, or emptiness. These are negative emotions suffered unnecessarily, as a way to torture ourselves with the feeling of what we do not have.

This in turn has the effect of making us feel bad about ourselves because, in the claim-to-power defense, we tend to believe that we do not get because of some kind of inner flaw, deficiency, or inappropriate behavior.

Working out these attachments is like learning a new language. The learning has to permeate beyond the intellectual layer into our emotions. We all have resistance to letting go of our feelings of being short-changed, and in so many people the resistance wins.

Feelings of being short-changed are relevant in what Freud termed "penis envy." To me, penis envy does not mean that women want to be men with a literal penis. Rather, it means that women can become entangled in the feeling of missing out on what the penis may represent to them—power, getting, control. As a woman develops her self-esteem, she no longer is caught in the feeling of missing out on the strength and authority symbolized by the penis.

In this oral context, it might be said generally that women have more emotional issues over the feeling of missing out on what someone else has (i.e. beauty, popularity, security), while men are more likely to become distressed over the prospect of losing what they already have (i.e. strength, potency, and possessions).

Creeping Orality

Orality, which refers to the consciousness of the baby, is everywhere in adult behavior and it is insidious. Oral issues creep around in economics, politics, culture, and lifestyles like spiders in the basement.

Oral issues lurk behind drug addiction, alcoholism, crime, promiscuity, eating disorders, shopping compulsion—yes, even the trade deficit and the national debt.

Orality is all about getting and not getting. The primary secret attachment in all of us is to the feeling of being deprived, refused, missing out, loss, denial, and not getting. Adults with oral conflicts have a "me-mine-more" mentality, which means they are self-centered and chronically dissatisfied with themselves and life.

Every baby's first oral frustration is the feeling of not getting and being refused when his or her wish for the breast or the bottle is not instantly fulfilled. Some children make poor internal adjustments to reality factors, and they grow up to be greedy, selfish, bored, dissatisfied, and worried about loss.

A fetus lives in a condition of prenatal bliss. Everything is provided through the mother's blood vessels. The fetus does not even have to breathe or swallow. Later behavior of the newborn reveals that he or she seeks a direct continuation of prenatal bliss.

Of course, we do not know what the fetus "thinks," if it thinks at all. Once born, however, we know the baby has a consciousness consisting of impressions, emotions, sensitivities, and drives.

In fact, to the newborn it feels as if he is a powerful wizard in the land of magical megalomania. It appears to the baby that whatever is happening—such as food appearing, objects coming before him, clothes being changed—is magically the result of his own wishes and powers.

Mom and Dad, and even objects, are just extensions of himself. Whatever happens is what he believes he wants. Everything given to him is self-given.

Everything that is refused hurts not only because of the deprivation, but also because it scrapes like sandpaper upon his fantasy of omnipotence, and this shows up in temper tantrums.

In his consciousness, he is not helpless in the world; rather, the world is an organ of his magic. This impression lingers even as we age. I clearly remember at age five being convinced I could magically replace my old baseball glove with a new one by hiding it in a secret place and wishing hard enough. It took months of coming back to that shabby glove before I was willing to give up my precious illusion.

A baby believes he is completely self-sufficient, and for a while he has difficulty accepting that an outer world even exists. It is not surprising a baby experiences this. What else would the baby know except his own little self? He has no knowledge of anything outside himself. There is no objectivity, no relativity, no perspective but to see himself as a little king at the center of existence. (Notice that a child often becomes the center of attention among adults, especially as adults identify with the child and revert unconsciously to being at the center.)

The story of the Garden of Eden can be seen as a metaphor for what we all experience, being expelled from the cozy womb into the cold world. The emotional health of a person depends on the degree to which he begins to accept this reality, or whether he or she continues to resist it and feel deprived and offended by it.

The child is able to resist reality by becoming convinced that all unpleasant experiences are products of his wishes. He does this by developing an unconscious affinity for (or attachment to) the feeling of being deprived, refused, denied, missing out, losing, or not getting. "Even though some experiences are unpleasant," the child's consciousness concludes, "I give it to myself, since everything I experience is a product of my wishes. Therefore, I must want it. It must be good."

The child now begins to acquire an expectation of, and an attachment to, the feeling of being deprived. One way a child, and later an adult, will pay a price in suffering for this attachment, as well as unconsciously defend against it, is *by becoming greedy, grasping, and selfish.* The inner defense proclaims, "No, it's not true I like being deprived: the problem is, I'm greedy."

Let's examine our culture where oral issues—attachments to deprivation, missing out, and loss—account for much anxiety, unhappiness, and self-defeat. With previous generations, the drive for survival consumed much physical and psychic energy. With more leisure, however, inner conflicts are not so easily repressed. Now, as we lay about with less to do, repressed oral conflicts intrude upon our prospects for fun and pleasure.

In this society, consumption has become the pillar supporting our economic system. People are often considered consumers first and citizens second. However, studies show that despite a doubling of per capita spending on personal consumption since the 1950s, people are no more happy now.

We are super-saturated with advertising, and shopping has become a primary cultural activity. That effect of advertising combined with our oral weaknesses have made us what we have become—a kind of sub-species of the noble citizen who have relegated old-fashioned virtues such as honesty, integrity, and dignity to the dead file of quaint remembrances as we scramble over one another on our way to the next bargain basement in mad celebration of life's commercialization.

Pervasive advertising usurps the emotional imagination to serve its own purpose. We become drawn to images or messages that play on our inner dissatisfactions. That means the visual drive or emotional imagination, when operating outside our awareness, tends to focus on the advertising message because of our unconscious willingness to flirt with feelings of loss, deprival, not getting, missing out, never having enough, never feeling satisfied, disappointment, and so on.

For those with low self-esteem, money and merchandise often become the primary indicators of personal worth. Some people feel that, "Without money, I'm nothing." Satisfaction comes from having more of it than others and from having more of it this year than last. Money, merchandise, and food are often indistinguishable to the unconscious—it's easy to feel emotionally deprived of one and all. These three elements substitute for the breast—for mother's milk, love, and nurturing.

The nation's biggest problem may be the existence of tens of millions of citizens who are out of touch with their own value and plagued by oral conflicts that cause them intense dissatisfaction with who they are and what they have. Instead of feeling gratitude, they feel starved. Instead of seeing the world with wonder, they see it with want. "Gotta have it!" is the advertising refrain of one national company.

This *want* is directly related to low self-esteem. In the first place, the person with plenty of self-esteem does not experience this intangible want, this longing or inner emptiness. Secondly, the individual experiencing deprival often rationalizes that he does not deserve to get because he is allegedly inadequate or inferior. Consider some of the ways that low self-esteem is expressed: "Nothing good ever happens to me" or "If only I had that, then I would be happy," or "Life is boring—nothing here interests me."

Many of us can remember Mom or Dad saying, "Why can't you appreciate what you have!" It irritated us to hear it then, and the memory of it irritates us now. We know we should appreciate what we have. But it is so hard when we are orally fixated and when advertising keeps showing us something bigger and better. Consequently, we see everything revolve around ourselves and our insecurities. We are desperate to cover up the oral attachments which produce insecurities and anxieties, and consumerism serves as a baby blanket or a soother to feel better about ourselves. If we had an economy in which consumerism were not the driving force, we might more easily find fulfillment in the search for love, commitment, friendship, community, art, beauty, and nature.

Instant gratification, we are told, brings the greatest pleasure. Many agree and want their oral satisfactions right away without going through the necessary work or preparation. So they resort to haste rather than mastery, image rather than substance, and debt instead of saving.

When we don't have money, we use credit, and instead of being masters of ourselves we become servants of our debt, and we have more reason to feel bad about ourselves.

Naive individuals believe that good feelings require the stimulus of external agents, events, or situations and that their bad feelings come from others or outside circumstances. Under this assumption, the siren song of materialism is irresistible, while validation from others makes them feel alive and successful.

Some observers have suggested that frugality or parsimony may become stylish in the 1990s. If such a trend were to develop, it might be a kind of "economic anorexia," an overreaction or adjustment to a previous excess. Unless the oral issues are examined and understood, chances are good that freewheeling consumer bingeing will make a comeback as we swing back and forth between extremes.

This does not mean, of course, that we have to turn away from abundance. But as long as the attachments to deprivation, refusal, and loss remain unrecognized, we will suffer from compelling greed, desires, dissatisfactions, and impatience. We will not be aligned with our best interests nor the well-being of the next generation as we bring down on ourselves dire economic consequences such as massive debt, poor quality production, squandered resources, and widespread pollution.

Our love affair with materialism relates directly to low self-esteem. When a person is not feeling good about himself, he is preoccupied emotionally with a sense of something missing. He is likely to be desperate for something that makes him feel better, and he is willing to become a major-league consumer, careless of his mounting debt, in his vain attempt to ease the crying need inside him.

Frankenstein Is Here

A major element in low self-esteem is the unconscious affinity for being reproached and condemned. People with low self-esteem often are involved with others in the give-and-take of malevolence and hatred. This self-defeating behavior either involves conflict with others or it takes the form of conflict within oneself, in the form of self-reproach, self-hatred, and self-condemnation. This harshness against one's own self is especially evident with addictive personalities.

One of my clients was homosexual and, as he told me, obsessed with sex. He masturbated two or three times every day. He could not refuse a sexual proposition. He was an addictive personality although abstinent from alcohol and drugs when he came to see me.

"It's worse than that," he said. "I carry condoms with me but I never use them. And I get in situations of very unsafe sex, and I snicker, I just laugh in the face of the danger. I say, 'Go ahead and kill me, I don't care.'

"Right at the moment of the greatest danger," he went on, "I get this devilish, sinister feeling, and I laugh like . . . it feels like it's not me!"

After these episodes, he said, he would become remorseful and fearful. "'Oh, you fool!' I say to myself. 'Why are you doing this? I can't believe I'm doing this!' And if I get AIDS, I know I'll kick and scream and ask why, why, why? I torment myself for days in a flood of self-reproach."

"Of course, this is very serious," I told him. "In the moment of your greatest danger, you are succumbing to the dark side of yourself. In the moment that your dark side takes over your ego, you get a rush, a thrilling high, that makes you feel all-powerful. You are feeding your egotism, and it has the effect of a drug, creating an all-powerful sense of yourself. You spit in the eye of death itself. It is exciting, exhilarating, to get in touch with such a sense of power. You are seduced by it because of your underlying sense of inadequacy and worthlessness.

"Later, when you come back to your senses, you are appalled at your behavior. And you are right—it is this other part of you that takes over and brings you to the brink of the horror of AIDS. Try to focus on the underlying weaknesses or attachments in your unconscious that make this feeling of all-powerfulness so appealing to you. Your weaknesses include your attachments to rejection and disapproval that create your low self-respect. We will keep working on this. You can see it's a matter of life and death.

"In the meantime, when you do something that you know is unwise and dangerous, try to resist the temptation to condemn yourself for it. Your problem is compounded by the degree to which you subsequently berate yourself. Sometimes people get involved in unwise activities mainly because of their unconscious and masochistic willingness to punish and condemn themselves afterwards."

Seldom have I heard the dark side of ourselves expressed so dramatically. With ingredients such as self-aggression, ignorance, masochism, and self-centeredness, this dark side generates our negativity from one thousand different recipes to produce humanity's smorgasbord of suffering and self-destruction.

"Everyone is a moon," wrote Mark Twain, and "has a dark side which he never shows to anyone." Often a person does not even see the dark side in himself. Many people catch only glimpses of it and quickly draw the curtains before they should see more. Even when they are smart enough to seek therapy, they can still only handle one peek at a time.

In 1920, in *Beyond The Pleasure Principle*, Freud introduced the concept of a dark side as a self-aggressive drive that he called the death drive, which is opposed to Eros, the life drive or Pleasure Principle. In 1930 in *Civilization And Its Discontents*, he stated that undischarged infantile aggression accumulates in the superego (which Edmund Bergler later identified as the hidden master of the personality). Freud realized that aggression is directed from the superego at one's own self or ego with as much severity as individuals act aggressively toward each other.

Let me state it another way. We are all born with aggression. It is needed to survive in the world. The aggression is aroused in the oral stage when reality presents a child with affronts to his megalomania (witness a child's temper tantrums). A child cannot expend all the aggression into the environment, mainly because of his weak musculature. However, aggression is a drive and has to go somewhere. It turns inward where it contributes to the formation of the superego, from where the aggression is later directed against one's own self in the form of self-reproach, self-hatred, and self-condemnation.

This harshness is like a Frankenstein monster because we ourselves create it out of our human nature, although quite inadvertently, and because it turns against our own self.

We are always trying to neutralize this force of self-aggression with excuses, illusions, lies, and other defenses. This is why, as Twain insightfully noted, "Man's sole impulse is the securing of his own self-approval." People torment themselves to their graves in futile pursuit of that approval. It was how we felt with our parents—never quite good enough.

Everyone has self-aggressive functioning to some degree. In the mildest cases, it accounts for how we limit ourselves, hold ourselves back, conform to the expectations of others, or think less of ourselves. In more serious cases, the self-aggression produces self-defeating and self-destructive behaviors that lead to accidents, health problems, and early death. It is amazing how humanity has covered up the operation of our self-aggression, this Watergate of the psyche.

Yet you can see it everywhere as children torment each other, parents abuse children, bosses tyrannize employees, spouses offend one another, and neighbors envy the Jones. I discussed this once with a psychologist who said, "I just can't bring myself to believe in this pessimistic view of ourselves." Notice that his viewpoint was based on his emotional—not scientific—considerations.

To see the dark side of our nature is to adopt a realistic—not a pessimistic—viewpoint. We want to see the negative to minimize it, not to dwell on it. Moreover, the existence of a dark side serves splendidly to accentuate the drama of our lives. Each person can feel a higher purpose in his quest for liberation from it.

There are ways to approach and understand this. For instance, what accounts for the human fascination with archvillains? Would not life be drab without adrenalin pumpers such as Darth Vadar, Lex Luthor, Capt. Nemo, Dr. Doom, Goldfinger, Capt. Hook, and the Phantom of the Opera? We flock to the movies to see various unrepentant monsters, aliens, Frankenstein creatures, Draculas, and everyday sociopathic killers. Their only goal in life is to find victims to abuse, to make us miserable for the sake of misery.

As the movie hero squashes these villains, viewers experience tremendous inner satisfaction and conscious delight. If only every movie-goer could do it to his own tormentor, that unsuspected inhabitant of his psyche, that harsh center of impersonal power that can overwhelm the low self-esteem individual with guilt, shame, fear, and doubt, and ultimately bring about his self-defeat or self-destruction.

Self-aggression is often experienced in the form of mocking or reproachful inner voices (from the inner conscience or superego). These inner voices first become operational when the child, in order to save face, makes an unconscious identification with the requirements and precepts of adults (coaxing, information, directives, admonition, exhortation, and punishment). In other words, the child exchanges the external warning voice of parents for an internal warning voice. Both voices say one and the same *don't.* But believing that the inner voice is self-chosen enables the child to save pride and preserve narcissism: "Nobody tells me what to do. I am the one who decides what to do and what not to do."

As stated earlier, the inner voice is not necessarily a direct result of negative parental messages. Whether his parents are loving or not, a child internalizes their directives and his inner voice takes up the harsh, severe, and punishing elements of the parents, while their loving side is not incorporated, apparently because of a child's tendency to believe and to take to heart the negative inferences or implications.

With low self-esteem, we are tempted to give credence to these voices expressing the following kinds of thoughts and self-defeating beliefs: "You just don't measure up," or "You can't even do the simple things right," or "Here you are still stuck in this," or "It's no wonder they don't approve of you." In a person's mind, the voices often are expressed in the first person, i.e. "I just don't measure up," or "I can't even . . ." or "I can't believe that . . ."

These critical voices leave people with the feeling, "No matter what I do, it's never good enough." For example, a man came into my office, pointed to his head and said, "I had a busy week upstairs here. I beat myself up verbally all week long." As a child, he had felt beaten up by his parents' disapproval. Of course, parents are often disapproving. But children also feel disapproval for what is simply normal parental child-raising. For example, the parents of a 13-year-old boy decide, in their judgment, that he is too young to go to an out-of-town concert. The boy interprets this to mean that they consider him to be too immature to handle the experience and that they do not trust him. He misinterprets the situation and cultivates feelings of disapproval.

Whether the sense of disapproval comes from insensitive parents, from a misunderstanding of parents' actions and intentions, or because the child becomes the parent to himself to preserve childish narcissism, the feeling is maintained into our adult life as the inner voice of self-reproach.

Many of my clients tell me that this voice bombards them every day, every hour, and sometimes it seems every minute. One man told me, "My inner voice is so powerful and crippling, it seems I am frozen in place. I can't seem to believe in myself anymore."

"It's important," I tell clients, "to *see and experience* these thoughts and beliefs as self-aggression. The inner voices of self-aggression compare metaphorically with having a demon on your shoulder, whispering detractions, gripes, worries, and various negative considerations in your ear. Those inner voices specialize in making you feel bad about yourself. It may feel impossible to stop the voices. But you can refrain from taking them seriously once you recognize your own self-defeating participation, that is your willingness to listen to those voices and take their messages to heart.

"This willingness is a result of your attachments to feeling criticized, deprived, controlled, rejected, or inadequate. One part of you will defend against the voices, trying to vouch for your better half, and this creates an internal dialogue with one part of you speaking on your behalf and the other part ready to squash you like a bug. Try to watch the self-denigration, observing it like an objective witness, seeing with what 'evidence' or ammunition it comes at you. See the extent to which you buy into it and want to take it seriously. Recognize your willingness to indulge in self-torture, to hurt yourself and berate yourself. See that you now reproach yourself as your parents once did, or as you feel they once did, only now you are even harder on yourself.

"It's a very nice feeling when your better half refrains from taking this self-aggression at face value. Then you no longer are emotionally distressed by the messages of this harsh inner conscience.

"In fact, feeling good about ourselves happens whenever the inner conscience stops attacking us, or when we learn to neutralize the attacks without resorting to self-damaging defenses. That's when we stop feeling the need to produce guilt and shame."

Often people try to beat back the accusations of the inner conscience ("You're no good, you've got no value, and everybody knows it") by chanting positive affirmations ("I am a success. I am a kind loving person"). Some people believe explicitly in the value of affirmations and are not aware that they are using them as defenses to ward off the accusations of the inner conscience. It is true that affirmations can temporarily silence the inner conscience and can produce a temporary feeling of well-being. But the good feelings do not last. Positive affirmations are like taking aspirin for arthritis; they temporarily alleviate the symptoms but do not bring about a permanent cure. Positive affirmations are not necessary once a person has acknowledged and understood the origins of this internal force of self-aggression and how he maintains it in his life. Once you recognize how you use minor imperfections and flaws in your character and behavior to torment yourself, self-esteem has the proper soil to grow. It is only when you "buy into" the self-reproach being delivered up by the inner conscience that you feel wrong about yourself and want to defend yourself.

When assailed by this side of ourselves, we will often peep and take satisfaction in seeing others suffer, lose, be humiliated, or defeated. In peeping this way, we defend with words such as, "I am not so inadequate or worthless. Look at that person! He's a bigger loser than me." Or, "Look at Greta Garbo in her final agony. I'm not nearly as pathetic."

Inner voices often make "a big deal" over the fact that you are failing to live up to your expectations of what you are supposed to be. These expectations (represented within the ego ideal) are a psychological formulation from childhood based on your infantile self-centeredness or megalomania and conceived to save face or preserve narcissism. The child takes expectations such as these very seriously: "When I grow up, I will be the strongest man in the world" or "I will be the most beautiful woman." Later in life, self-aggression now tortures this adult with the discrepancies between his present circumstances and the still-enshrined expectations of his ego ideal: "How come you're not as special as you thought you were, you worthless drone? How come you're not doing great things?"

In the unconscious or semi-conscious dialogue, the self defends against these inner accusations with a thousand excuses: "Life is too hard, I didn't have any luck, too many people let me down." But, at best, these defenses only temporarily neutralize the self-aggression. Your pound of flesh is paid for every day by the guilt, shame, and dissatisfaction you experience under the onslaught of this self-aggression.

It may be that the single most significant source of unhappiness is the feeling of disapproval from the accusing or condemning inner voices. Consequences of this are frequent feelings of guilt, inadequacy, and failure. Through the defenses that we employ, we are willing to plead guilty to being flawed, defective, or inadequate in order to cover up our passive role or secret collusion in feeling criticized or condemned. To make the defenses work, we then have to believe in our alleged inadequacies—and feelings of guilt, shame, and low self-esteem follow behind us like haunting twilight shadows.

As with Einstein's Theory of Relativity, we have trouble grasping this concept. It becomes clear, however, as we begin to work with it on our personal issues. Unlike the Theory of Relativity, much more is at stake. There is a great need for humanity to comprehend the operations of the unconscious mind.

We cannot conquer the dark side by pretending it does not exist, although we have been trying to deny it for centuries. One does not become enlightened by imagining figures of light, said Carl Jung, but by making the darkness conscious.

Violence wins no points against the Frankenstein monster within. Commitment, humility, and courage are the battle flags under which we must proceed; so the engagement brings out the best in us.

Forbidden Sights

A child experiences doubt and uncertainty about himself when he is told or made to understand that he cannot look at certain things, especially mother's breasts or father's penis.

In weaning, the child has been refused the breast. Next, he or she is not even allowed to look at it. To do so is bad and naughty. But the child's profound self-centeredness makes him feel entitled to have whatever he wants, whatever he sees. He feels he is being refused. Inner conflicts are created.

Soon he is aware that Mommy and Daddy have secret lives in the bathroom and their bedroom. Seeing what goes on there is not allowed. He knows he would like to look. What are they up to? Why are the sights forbidden to him?

Using his imagination, he begins to peep. He peeps into the darkness of what is forbidden, trying to shed light on this world that is closed to him. It is thrilling for him to imagine what must be going on—though he feels wrong or guilty for doing so.

Perhaps he walks into a room and sees Mommy nursing baby sister. Mommy tells him to get out—watching this is forbidden. She makes him feel ashamed for wanting to look. He walks in on Daddy in the bathroom and is told, perhaps angrily, to get out. He begins to feel that parents are mean and sight-depriving. The more he feels controlled and deprived, the more he will want to peep and the more excited he will become in the act of peeping.

If you remember being embarrassed seeing someone of the opposite sex nude, it is because you felt caught doing something forbidden. I remember at age nine being in a bunk-house with two men at the mine near where I lived in Nova Scotia, and suddenly spying on the wall a calendar poster of a naked woman. The impact on me was instantaneous and powerful. I blushed, frozen in anxiety, then looked down at the floor.

I could not bring myself to look again at the poster, although if I had been alone in the room I surely could not have resisted. As my heart raced and my mind buzzed, I was acutely sensitive to the feeling that the men were watching me closely.

Alone, my eyes would have soaked up that pin-up girl. But in front of the men, the injunction of the forbidden was overpowering. If I had dared to peep in front of them, I was certain they would say, "You bad boy! You really like that, don't you, looking at what you are not supposed to see. We can see how excited you become looking at what is forbidden. For shame!"

My anxiety and my hesitation to look at the pin-up girl covered up my secret attachment to the thrill of being caught and punished for being naughty. I was only aware at the time, though, of feeling confused and bad about myself.

Try sitting on a crowded beach with a pair of binoculars, and begin to look through the binoculars at the lovely scantily-clad bodies strolling by. If you are relatively normal, you will immediately feel uncomfortable doing this. Suppose, as you take in the magnification of some opposite-sexed hunk strolling toward you, this person looks right at you. Suddenly, you feel mortified.

That is because, in using the binoculars, the act of peeping is accentuated. With the binoculars, you are no longer just a casual observer passively taking in the sights, able to claim that you are not peeping but just hanging out. The binoculars identify you as an active peeper. This is definitely naughty, and you will expect that person whose bosoms or buns you are magnifying to be annoyed, if not disgusted, with you.

Compare it to sitting anonomously on the beach, lusting after sexy people from behind your dark sunglasses. No problem here. No one can see your eyes. No one knows you are peeping. No one can catch you. You feel secure.

With passive peeping behind sunglasses, it is much easier to defend against the inner accusation of wrongdoing. "I am not actively peeping," the unconscious defense contends, "it's these people in all their boldness who are exhibiting themselves to me."

Remember, a person on the beach may be using his voyeurism for the sheer appreciation of beauty. He is only a negative peeper if he is using his visual drive to feel deprived and lusting after what is unavailable to him, or if he is being judgmental of others, or feeling less than others, or if he is feeling himself to be under their influence in some way.

Creative artists are voyeuristic. They succeed on the basis of the quality of their visual drive. When their creativity is blocked, their visual drive is impaired, often because of inner injunctions against the use of the imagination which is equated with forbidden peeping.

Mark Twain in his autobiography described the uninhibited voyeuristic instincts of the artist. He told of a time in his youth when, with a man named Hicks, he was on stage trying to fool an audience into believing he had been hypnotized:

"Hicks had no imagination; I had a double supply. He was born calm, I was born excited. No vision could start a rapture in him and he was constipated as to language, anyway; but if I saw a vision I emptied the dictionary onto it and lost the remnant of my mind into the bargain." Twain obviously had no injunctions against creative peeping.

Creative or positive peeping is blocked not only in artists but in millions of ordinary people. As children, many of us were discouraged from seeing into the reality of things. "Look at that fat lady!" the child exclaims, to be told by an adult, "Shush, you are not supposed to say (see) that!" Or, "Look how miserable Daddy is all the time. Shouldn't I say something about that?" The answer we get, directly or indirectly, is *no*; we must not say it or even see it. As part of *The Great Law* (see "Passivity and Shame"), we learn over and over *not* to see certain things. The feeling is that to *really see* is to see something bad (or to look bad to others for seeing it). Now when you have the chance to look into yourself (your unconscious) to see important truths that can set you free, you are discouraged by the fear that what you see will be bad or shameful.

Adults who easily blush are engaged in negative peeping, looking for someone to look down on them. Blushing is an exhibitionistic defense that contends, "I do not want to peep; on the contrary, the problem is that I am guilty of showing myself." This illustrates the readiness some of us have to overemphasize the active or aggressive component (in this case, "I exhibit") in order to cover up the more deeply rooted passivity of being secretly attached to feeling caught and punished by the eyes of others for "naughty" behavior.

This is tricky, so I will repeat the last paragraph in different words. Blushing anticipates punishment. Someone who blushes has been caught red-handed peeping. Here is how it works: I look up and peep at you, meaning I am imagining (based on transference) that you and your eyes are seeing me in some deficiency. My secret here is to be getting off passively on the feeling of you looking at me, putting me on the spot, for some alleged inadequacy or wrongdoing on my part. To defend against this, I call attention to myself by blushing, so that in this claim to power I can say I cause you to look at me with those judgmental eyes: "I do not want to peep; I want to show myself." In exhibiting, however, I feel bad about myself for looking foolish.

The blusher is always anticipating punishment, and he blushes when his guilt (and hence the anticipation of punishment) is intimated. One individual, the son of a minister, blushed in church when his father preached against sin. He felt exposed for his "misdeeds." His misdeeds, however, were only acted out in his imagination via peeping.

The opposite of the blusher is the critical peeper whose impulse to catch others doing something "bad" operates on a hair-trigger.

In summary, low self-esteem can have origins in the experience of feeling bad or wrong for wanting to see and experience elements of life which we believe and discover to be forbidden. (The sense that peeping is forbidden does not have to be imparted by parents.) Inner conflict is created in trying to resist the desire or compulsion to peep, and the individual feels shame and guilt which translate into a sense of being wrong or flawed as a person.

Fear of Fear Itself

People with low self-esteem are often ruled by their fears. Sometimes their emotional imaginations are completely out of control, and they are tormented with visualizations of precisely what they do not want to see, as in the case of phobics.

Phobics often try to avoid what they fear, but their fears come to life in the emotional imagination like creepy-crawlies in a nightmare.

Dorothy, a businesswoman, had become fearful of driving. While driving, she became convinced emotionally she would lose control of the vehicle, crash, and be killed. Whenever possible, she drove with her cruise control on because then she felt that the car was in control.

At one point, Dorothy stopped driving but she continued to experience graphic visualizations of being out of control behind the wheel, crashing, and killing herself and others.

In therapy, she revealed her business was in financial difficulty and on the verge of failing. Dorothy blamed herself and felt she had caused the setback. She was entangled in feelings of helplessness and powerlessness with respect to her business, and was convinced emotionally the business situation was out of control and that she would wreck it eventually.

Dorothy displaced her emotional states onto driving where her sense of impending doom came together with her alleged ineptitude, powerlessness, and feelings of being out of control.

Part of the problem was the degree to which she identified with her business. Dorothy's self-esteem and personal validation hinged on her business success, raising the emotional stakes as her business failed.

In therapy, she became aware of these previously unconscious conflicts and identifications. Dorothy began to climb out of the feelings of helplessness and the emotional conviction of her own ineptitude. Soon she was driving with confidence and handling business problems with more ease.

The emotional imagination is a major component in phobias, and phobias are all about fears. So what are fears all about?

It is normal to be afraid if your airplane suddenly starts to dive out of the sky, or you wake up and see a burglar climbing in the bedroom window. But what accounts for someone's fear of heights when the person has never fallen from a significant height? Or why is someone afraid to leave his house and walk down the street in his quiet neighborhood?

The problem starts with baby fears that can persist throughout our lives. These include fear of being starved, created by the offense that mother was not there instantly with food. Being devoured is another baby fear, a projection of the child's own aggressive designs upon the breast or bottle. Other baby fears include fear of being dropped, fear of being choked, fear of being drained, and fear of castration.

When baby fears are not outgrown, they become part of the psyche's self-defeating substructure. In general, anxiety arises, then fear, when a person's defenses become ineffective in neutralizing the harshness of one's self-aggression. Our psychological defenses are complex and people are fooled by them. In one of these defenses, inner fears are projected outward. Now the danger appears to be external, and fears take on a sense of being validated or justified by factors in the environment. In other words, neurotic fears take on the apparent attributes of "reality" fears.

This is the mechanism of paranoia as well as phobia. In hypochondria, the fear is projected onto an organ or aspect of the body, and the person is convinced a health problem exists or he "self-creates" a health problem.

Fear of flying is a common phobia. The fearful individual is quick to visualize scenes in which he is crashing in a plane. If he sees a TV report about a crash, he identifies with the victims and feels their terror. If he plans to take a flight, he sees motors and wings falling off in his dreams.

Fear of flying often has more to do with unconscious fears of failing, being let down or disappointed by others, not trusting others. One client had felt let down and disappointed by his father. He was not consciously aware of the degree to which he still carried around those feelings, and ended up transposing the expectation of being let down (crashing) onto airline pilots. As this individual worked out his conflict with his father, his fear of flying ceased to be a problem.

In another example, an individual was afraid to be alone. If left alone, she experienced panic attacks (dizziness, heart palpitations, trembling, and fear of dying). She also had a driving phobia involving fear of having an accident on an isolated road. In therapy, she realized how much she still felt the loss of her mother's affection. She felt abandoned by her parents who, it seemed to her, were still rejecting her by not helping with her children and not being there for her. She also saw her husband as unsympathetic, even though he appeared to be trying his best to please her.

Her fear of an accident on an isolated road was heightened as she identified unconsciously with her children. She became entangled in feeling how abandoned her children would feel if such an unfortunate incident were to occur.

Her underlying problem was her unconscious readiness to believe that no one cared for her. She imagined herself alone and deserted, becoming entangled in feelings of abandonment. She countered this by feeling the need to have someone present all the time. In therapy, as she sorted out these previous unconscious attachments, and saw how her emotional imagination was used to stoke them, her insecurities became less threatening.

Five kinds of fears are common among phobics. The five are (i) fear of being abandoned (as in previous example), (ii) fear of being criticized and judged, (iii) fear of being shamed and humiliated, (iv) fear of losing control, and (v) fear of rejection. Each of these fears leaves people feeling deficient and inadequate.

Notice in all five of these fears that, beneath the surface, the individual is secretly attached to that which he fears. Irrational fears serve as defenses to cover up the secret attachments. For instance, a person with an attachment to abandonment would say, "Look at how scared I am of the prospect of being abandoned. I am *not* secretly looking for that feeling." Phobics pay a great price in suffering for using various fears as defenses against their secret attachments.

Here is an example of number two, fear of being criticized and judged. One social phobia is the inability to urinate in a public washroom. A man with this problem told me, "When I stand at the urinal, I want to turn and look over my shoulder to see who's watching me. The feeling is that anyone watching will be smirking at me for not being able to perform."

This man, a salesman, had performance anxiety in other areas of his life. When his boss was watching him, he had more trouble relating well to customers and feeling comfortable with them. When the boss was absent, he was able to make the best of his communication skills.

Not being able to urinate in a public washroom, nor being able to sell cars when the boss is looking, is negative exhibitionism. The person's problem begins with the peeping, in this case looking over his shoulder (literally or figuratively) to see or imagine someone watching him unable to perform.

The individual now defends unconsciously against his passive attachment to this feeling by saving face with this claim to power: "No, no! I'm not looking to passively experience being looked at as an inadequate performer. I cause it to happen. People look at me because I mess up; I do it wrong. I'm too nervous and uptight. That's my problem."

A man's performance anxiety can manifest as sexual impotence. The gentleman stands in front of his lady with a limp penis, watching her looking at him with disappointment and displeasure. In that moment, the man is (i) secretly indulging in the feeling of being seen as a wimp (weak, inadequate, unsatisfactory); (ii) identifying with the woman's feelings of being refused, deprived, or disappointed; and (iii) consciously feeling shamed and embarrassed.

Pseudo-patriotism is another condition of fear. It is a displacement of dependence from the authority of mother and father onto a nation. The pseudo-patriot is too insecure to stand alone in the comfort of his own being, so he identifies with the might of the whole and cuddles up in the bosom of national security. One of his defenses is to assume a superior posture which can become, on a large scale, petty nationalism.

In this modern society, if you have enough money or someone to support you, you can try to hide from your fears in your house or your apartment. Locked in your own little world, your fears will grow into concrete ogres and you will become an agoraphobic who feels dizzy and gets heart palpitations just in imagining yourself walking down the street.

An agoraphobic is one who, in a distortion of his emotional imagination, produces visualizations and rationalizations enhancing and promoting the dangers in his environment. In his avoidance of those "dangers," he is like a mole afraid of the light, so scared that he is afraid of what can set him free.

Some people have a great fear of losing money, especially among those with a lot of it. These people have invested their sense of self in money and the trappings of money and power, and to be without it feels to them like annihiliation. They are emotional and obsessive about maintaining their financial strength because they are lacking the security that comes from inner strength. Without their wealth, it feels to them that they have nothing to fall back on. They tend to use their wealth in a way that promotes a superior self-image and that masks an underlying sense of inferiority. A confident person does not need external crutches to feel his worth. Of course, money and wealth are desirable in themselves. The problem is that some individuals are attached emotionally to money in a way that causes them grief and limits their personal development.

Freedom from fear and phobias mean inner liberation from the unresolved conflicts and secret attachments of your psyche. Dealing with fear means moving into the fear. If you do not get the best of your fears, they will get the best of you.

Life is not a guaranteed annuity. There is no security that a baby is aware of when he or she is pushed out of the womb by the force of nature. Life is always pushing people to grow and often that feels scary.

Bad Little Girl

When Julie was eight years old, her mother made her wear "a silly babyish dress" to school. There the kids ridiculed the dress and made fun of her.

While her dress was being mocked, Julie felt as if the essence of herself—every hair on her head and dream in her heart—were being mocked. She came home from school and told her mother what had happened. "Oh, that's ridiculous!" her mother exclaimed. "We'll show them! You're going to wear that dress again tomorrow!"

Later, as an adult, Julie carried within herself the readiness to imagine that other people saw her as somehow foolish or inappropriate. She developed a social phobia—fear of being at parties or weddings.

At parties, she would peep, secretly looking for people to be looking back at her with mocking eyes and critical expressions. Even when no one took notice of her, she would imagine in her extreme self-consciousness that they were thinking ill of her, or that they would think ill of her should they at any moment glance her way. (The event with her mother and the dress did not "make" Julie into a social phobic. Another girl in the same situation might have taken the experience in stride.)

She was familiar with the feeling of being shamed. Although she had done nothing specifically "bad," she carried within herself the fear of being exposed and found out. She defined exposure as the feeling of others seeing into her soul, where she bore an inner sense of somehow being unworthy, unacceptable, and bad.

Many of us, were we required to stand naked before the eyes of a crowd, would feel ashamed of our bodies and, consequently, of our own selves. Yet, in the innocence of being seen as we are, what is there really to be ashamed of?

The shame seems to come instantaneously. But it is preceded by peeping in the instant when one looks into the eyes of others expecting to see those eyes looking back with disapproval, criticism, or rejection.

A person can cover up a secret attachment to being seen in this negative light by believing that he is bad for the exhibitionism (even if it only amounts to him standing around feeling that he looks silly or out of place). The shame now represents the acceptance of guilt and punishment for the so-called exhibitionism, the act of doing something to call negative attention to oneself, or the condition of being "imperfect" (fat, skinny, ugly, nervous, awkward) as to draw attention to oneself.

Sometimes the exhibitionism is perverse as well as self-defeating. The voyeur (the one who catches others doing something "bad" to try to prove he is not secretly attached to being seen negatively) could become a sexual exhibitionist, a playground flasher for instance, using a claim-to-power defense that he, of his own free will, causes people to look at him negatively. He then indirectly experiences his own secret attachment by identifying with the shame and embarrassment that others experience in looking upon him in his act of exhibitionism.

What is the low self-esteem person thinking and feeling when he goes to a party? The more this person's emotional imagination works against him, the more he goes to parties to peep and to exhibit. The more his visual drive is working well, the more he goes to a party to take in visual, verbal, and other pleasures.

"Go to your party to see and not to be seen," I once told a client, and he looked relieved and amazed, as if he had just heard the secret of the universe.

The person who goes to peep and be seen risks having a miserable time. What if others do not pay attention to him or, worse, purposely avoid him? How disappointed does he become if certain special people are not there at the party? And if an enemy or two shows up, will he obsess negatively on them? One client told me, "I always search the party for someone who looks better than me."

The person who goes to have fun is not dependent on how he is being seen by others, nor will his fun be spoiled if certain people are absent or present. This is because, with his eyes, he takes in what is available and what looks most appealing for his own pleasure, and avoids peeping at what might inflame a negative reaction.

Imagine a Mad Hatter's tea party where every person is going around wondering what everyone else is thinking of him or her. In their self-consciousness, everybody would be projecting and bouncing their own insecurities off the faces and imaginations of everybody else like coyotes on peyote. It happens all the time.

Maureen, a 30-year-old computer programmer, became convinced in her twice-weekly college computer class that a certain man was looking at her a lot. This man flirted with the women in the class, and she often felt that, while the teacher was speaking, this man was observing her with interest. Maureen only had to turn her head ninety degrees to see whether the man was indeed looking at her. But she had not looked to verify her hunch.

That was because she did not want to see that the man might *not* be looking at her. In this class, Maureen was a peeper. One of her priorities, when looking at others in the class, was to find evidence of the degree to which they were not interested in her. She had not made any friends there, and she was repeating her experience of high school when she had felt rejected and overlooked by her fellow students. To cover up her secret willingness to replay this feeling from her past, she needed a defense. Her defense became her emotional conviction that at least this man was interested in her. This defense collapsed when, during a class break, the man passed right in front of her to talk excitedly to another woman.

"I just stood there, feeling invisible," Maureen said, "and I went back to class and was in such an emotional state I hardly heard a word the teacher said. Then I went home and cried for half an hour." She had not made any attempts to make friends in this class because her self-defeating side was willing to re-experience the old hurts and familiar feelings of being rejected and ignored.

Gloria was another client with a peeping problem. She weighed 160 pounds and intensely disliked her body. "I have a horrible body image," she told me. "In my aerobics class, I can't even stand to glance in the mirror at myself."

While Gloria disliked her body, she dressed very well and tried to look good for others. Consciously, it was very important that she look her best, but unconsciously she was quick to indulge in the feeling that others saw her as "bad" or unworthy. Gloria remarked, "A woman at work said she thought I was overdressed, and I felt just awful, that she was seeing right through me, exposing who I really was."

She had been bulimic and was now in recovery, but maintained her weight at the upper range of what she considered acceptable. As a youngster, she had been teased by her peers for being chubby. "I don't even have to look at my body to feel bad about myself," Gloria said. "I can just visualize it. Or I can jump into other people's heads and imagine them looking at me."

A week earlier, she had had a panic attack as she became engrossed in the fantasy of being fired from her job for becoming too fat. The panic attack consisted of heart palpitations, sweaty palms, dizziness, and trembling, as well as vivid and constant visualizations of the dreaded event. Without the advantage of insight and therapy, Gloria would be likely to gain weight and act out what she feared the most and what she was secretly attached to—being rejected for her "unacceptable" body and her "unworthiness."

Guilt is another expression of low self-esteem. One writer found after interviewing 1,000 working women that guilt was their greatest emotional problem. "It saddened me to realize that the present generation of working mothers, the beneficiaries of so much hope and striving, were haunted by such conflict," the writer reflected.

Among the guilt-producing issues listed were: going back to work, taking a leave of absence, leaving the office early to attend a school play, working late and missing dinner, being in too stressful a job, not earning enough, earning more than the husband, being short-tempered with the children, not disciplining more.

In all the above cases, the guilt (the feeling of deserving punishment) is misplaced. The women are feeling guilty for a surface symptom—some alleged wrongdoing. But the guilt belongs elsewhere. Take the example of leaving the office early to attend a school play. Of course, this is not wrong in itself. But the woman may be imagining that her co-workers or

her boss are upset at her for leaving early. She would then be
flirting with feeling disapproved of. It is her unconscious
entanglement in feeling disapproval that produces the guilt.
When the guilt arises into her consciousness, she begins to
question or doubt her action in leaving early. In other words,
there was nothing wrong with leaving early to attend the play
but because she began to indulge in feeling disapproved of
for doing so, she created guilt which left her confused and
in doubt about herself.

The following is another example. Neil felt guilty and bad
about himself because he was unhappy with his wife's appearance. If only she were better looking, he kept saying to himself. This concern reflected his own insecurity. If his wife were
beautiful, then others would be more impressed with him for
having a beautiful wife. If she were just plain, he felt this was
a reflection on how he himself was seen by others. Neil could
also imagine that his wife was feeling inferior because she
was not beautiful. He would then identify with her in that
feeling, whether in fact she felt that way or not. He believed
his guilt was due to his selfishness for not accepting his wife
as she was—but the feeling of guilt was really produced in his
unconscious because he was using a subjective assessment of
his wife, produced in his emotional imagination, to indulge
in feeling inadequate and unworthy.

This last case illustrates another consequence of low self-
esteem. A client had been convinced that her husband's rov-
ing eye for other women was a sign of her inadequacy. She also feared he would leave her because of her alleged inadequacy, and so she had an operation to have her breasts en-
larged. The excellent results provided her husband with some
temporary amusement, but he soon returned to form, his
eyes as eager as ever to devour other shapely women. His
problem had nothing to do with her, and everything to do
with his own tendency to create ways to feel deprived and

denied. However, because of her low self-esteem she was convinced emotionally that she was the problem. After her husband left her, she sought out psychotherapy and began to work out her attachments to feeling unrecognized and unworthy.

Peeping at the Kids

When my emotional imagination is on the rampage, I make life tough on others too. I used to prowl around our house like a sharp-eyed wolf, looking for messes, dirt, or damage made by our children. And I still have not lost the knack, though I keep it on a shorter leash.

"There's nothing wrong with keeping a clean house and minimizing wear-and-tear," I said to myself. But my eye can spy a misplaced paper clip forty feet away. And how I could suffer when I saw a pillow out of place, or a paper cup on the living room coffee table, or a shoe on the dining room rug.

That the sight of one misplaced paper clip should feel like I had stuck it in my eye tells you something about peeping. Righteous indignation and sometimes throaty groans accompanied my spy missions around the house. Yes, I remember how my mother hounded me about the evil of things left lying around and sent me off with steel wool upon our hardwood floors on search-and-clean missions every Saturday morning. And I have been conditioned to pass the legacy of good housekeeping onto the next generation. It has nothing to do with promoting their self-esteem. It has to do with my unconscious willingness to resurrect that old feeling of being wrong and bad.

A parent usually subjugates his children to the same treatment he passively endured as a child. Of course, he does this unconsciously. If he felt ridiculed, he will be inclined to ridicule his kids; if he felt ignored, he will be inclined to ignore them; if he felt he had someone hovering over him with disapproval, ready to punish him for every misplaced rubberband, he will . . . well, you know. (In other cases, people go to the other extreme. For instance, someone who felt ignored as a kid may become overly attentive to his own kids, but in the process leave his kids feeling intruded upon or not trusted to act independently.)

As a child endures certain unpleasant feelings involving a parent, he says to himself, "I will never do this to my kids." But the unconscious does not keep those promises.

Many times I have stood in the doorways to my kids' bedrooms and felt my life reduced to the shambles before my eyes. How could they be so nonchalant, so indifferent to the importance of appearance? I saw them looking quizzically back at me as if I did not know, with all my worldly experience, the importance of what I stood for.

Little did I know, although I am sure they sensed it, that all I stood for was the promotion of self-suffering.

Seeing the internal promotion of one's own self-torture can be real tricky. The psychological defenses have to be penetrated, as the following case illustrates. Several times, for instance, when I thought I was catching my stepson being "bad," I was really playing mother to myself, putting myself back in that old childhood feeling through my identification with him.

For example, I often caught him failing to rinse out the dishes properly before putting them in the dishwasher. But in the moment I caught him, I was also catching myself. How do I know I was catching myself? By the intensity of my negative feelings. If I was simply after him to do a better job, I would be calm and reasonable with him because that would get the best results, especially if he were feeling controlled or criticized and was therefore passive-aggressively resisting the requirement to do his chores adequately.

In those moments when I caught him, I overreacted emotionally. I was identifying with him, thereby slipping into the feelings of having been caught myself doing something bad and being punished verbally. Then I covered up my secret attachment—my own willingness to re-experience those old feelings of being caught and punished—by blaming him for being bad.

I was imagining: "My mother would be outraged to see me putting such dirty dishes in the dishwasher. Would she ever let me have it!" My unconscious badgered me, "Wouldn't you like to be the one who has done that? Wouldn't you like to be bawled out and catch hell?"

"No, no," my unconscious ego defended, "not true at all. I'm like my mother. I'm going to overdo it. I'm going to yell and scream and make *him* look bad."

So to cover up my attachment to being caught and punished, I became testy with my stepson, believing I was justified for my disapproval of him. Then he reacted with anger, and soon I was feeling badly for having started an uproar. I became aware of looking bad in front of him and the rest of the family, feeling guilty for being the policeman and over-reacting, and the guilt I felt was the result—my punishment for peeping, although I attributed the guilt to my nasty over-reaction.

Some people feel that unless they do something exceptional, they are not really worth anything. Often these individuals were raised in families where recognition or validation was offered only when a child displayed practical ability and performed well in some capacity. Much of the time the child felt disapproved of. Little honor and respect were accorded simply for the sake of the child's own being.

Jean, a client in her early forties, experienced anxiety in her new position as leader of a group for compulsive overeaters. "I really feel I have to deliver," she said. "I feel pressure to fix them, to give them something that will work. Otherwise, I obsessively question my worth."

Jean had grown up with a demanding, controlling mother who never seemed satisfied with her. "When Mom came in the room," she said, "I would think, what does she want of me, do I look okay, what can I do right now to make everything okay? Mom was always looking me over, scrutinizing me, and never being satisfied."

In the mother's self-centeredness, she peeped at her child. She saw her own child only in relation to what she believed little Jean should be doing for her, or what she believed Jean was not doing for her, or how Jean was imperfect. The mother saw Jean, not as a separate and unique being, but as if she were looking upon some deficient part of her own self. It felt to the mother that she could maintain her emotional equilibrium by making Jean act and be a certain way. But this could not possibly work, and Jean was seen as the problem, the one who was deficient. Her mother projected onto Jean all that was deficient in herself. Her daughter was not seen for who she was. Instead she was seen in distortion, a creature of the mother's emotional imagination. This left Jean, who became an addictive personality, desperately entangled in her mother's narcissism and low self-esteem.

"I remember my birthday parties," Jean said, "my mother would take at least 100 black and white pictures of me. She had me stand this way and that way, every which way, while she snapped all those pictures. It felt like she had to get the perfect picture, and anything less was worthless." She added, "Now, when I look at a woman's face, all I look for are imperfections. If I spot any facial hair, that's where I focus, that's all I can see."

Jean learned that the best strategy to raise her self-esteem involved seeing how she peeped at others, looking for imperfections and then identifying through those she peeped at with the feeling of being seen as inadequate. Raising her self-esteem also involved deepening her awareness of her unconscious willingness to indulge in feeling criticized and seen as inadequate. She began to recognize the unconscious part of her that was attached to these negative feelings and was always ready to experience them again in some new context. Jean saw how sensitive she was to being criticized, even in situations where no criticism was implied, and realized how these emotional reactions served as defenses against her attachment to criticism. She began to see how she had misinterpreted other situations as reflections on her unworthiness, and how she had reacted defensively and angrily as a protest to cover up her collusion in the experience.

Critical Peeping

Haunting the nation's homes and byways is a breed of person who combines a judgmental mentality and a busybody imagination into a unique compulsion called critical peeping.

This peeping can be understood as the visual component in the compulsion to be judgmental. Unless you are a judge and get paid for it, being judgmental of others serves no good purpose. Such a mentality indicates low self-esteem and only causes you to suffer.

Dale, a retired older gentleman, lived in the same town as his teenage grandson. Dale's daughter, Gloria, had raised her son with a conscious effort to avoid the kind of focus on work and household chores that she felt her father had rigidly imposed on her. The boy was smart and self-assured. However, he did only a minimum of chores around his house and no work at all for his grandfather.

Dale had a very difficult time accepting the boy's nonchalant attitude to work. After mowing the grass and doing other work in his yard, Dale often came into his house muttering and moaning about his lazy grandson.

Gloria's mother told her that Dale often paced up and down the hallways protesting about the "spoiled" younger generation and his own grandson in particular. "The lazy bum," Dale would complain, "I can see him now—I just bet he's lying around doing absolutely nothing."

Raised on a farm, Dale had often worked from dawn to dusk helping his parents maintain it. In his family, hard work was the greatest virtue and shirking duties was equated with being bad and worthless. Dale still struggled with his own feelings of being devalued and worthless, and he was tempted to pin those feelings onto his grandson. His critical peeping, however, caused him suffering because, as he pointed a finger at his grandson, he was plunged via identification back into feelings of being bad and worthless himself.

Linda, owner of a dry-cleaning business, was another critical peeper. She said in her first session, "It bothers me terribly having to look upon my husband's body."

He had once weighed 300 pounds and had reduced his weight to 190 when they married. But his weight was creeping back up. He had on his body what she described as "quite a few unsightly stretch marks."

Linda's mother used to go through the family garbage, "looking for dirt" on the kids. When the mother did laundry, she examined the contents of their pockets, saying "I do the laundry, I'm entitled to look."

Now Linda was the one looking for dirt. She saw it on her customers at her dry-cleaning establishment, and it appeared to her as the imperfections on her husband's body. She identified with her husband when she looked at his stretch marks, feeling the embarrassment she imagined he would feel knowing he was being critically evaluated.

Her mother had always embarrassed easily, Linda remembered. "Mother once said to me, 'Just read this book about sex and don't ask me any questions.'"

Linda participated in amateur theater and recently had felt "very nervous and embarrassed" while singing to the audience. "I don't like people to stare at me too long," she said, adding that she had trouble making eye contact. When she was six years old, she peed her pants in front of kids who laughed at her for it. At eight, she remembered feeling mortified when kids pulled down her bathing suit at a public pool. Now she looked at her husband's naked body with the eyes of a critic. She once had been overweight herself but had become trim and attractive. Her mother had sent her to charm school for a few years so Linda would be sure to "look good."

"Looks were everything in our family," she remembered. "It was so important to my parents that our house looked perfect—with the lawn and plants and shrubs—so everyone who passed by would be impressed."

Linda looked at herself with the same critical eyes she cast upon her husband. She assumed others would look at her with her own eyes, meaning she expected others would be looking for dirt when they looked at her. She was preoccupied with the feeling that her parents disapproved of her for marrying beneath her class and for the career she had chosen. As a defense against her unresolved attachment to this feeling, she became the peeper looking for dirt on others.

She found herself being upset with her husband's table manners, especially when company was present. When the guests had left, she would lecture him on the importance of showing more class. Playing Amy Vanderbilt covered up her attachment to being seen by others in the manner in which she imagined they saw her husband. In lecturing him, she was also giving to her husband the disapproval she had felt from her mother, another aspect of her defense against being seen as bad or inadequate.

Often she looked at other men, saying to herself, "I wish my husband were like them. Why isn't he more important, a Fortune 500 businessman instead of a supermarket manager?" Her wish that he were more important covered up her attachment to the feeling that others saw him as unimportant and unworthy, and thereby also saw her as less worthy and unacceptable.

In summary, Linda peeped at others to find the dirt on them, as a defense against her own attachment to being seen critically. Unconsciously, however, the peeping became a vehicle whereby she identified with those caught and exposed by her visual acuity, as vicariously she re-experienced her old attachment to being seen in that negative light.

Behind every critical peeper is an injustice collector. This individual alleges that he is looking for injustices in order to expose them. But he is really interested in experiencing his secret attachments, which are fueled by his perception of real or alleged injustices, and he uses his emotional imagination to produce these experiences *ad infinitum.*

The classic injustice collector is pinned to his bed of nails by his oral fixation. Unaware of his leading role in creating his own suffering, he provokes a situation in which he is (or feels) denied or refused. He then reacts with righteous indignation and seemingly in his self-defense, while unconsciously indulging in feeling victimized.

If you recognize yourself as a critical peeper, first try to catch yourself in the act of looking at (or imagining) something that stirs up a negative reaction within you. Try to understand that you are doing this for an unconscious purpose, namely to engage in feelings of being refused, denied, rejected, criticized, or controlled. Next, monitor yourself as you catch yourself (or observe yourself) in the act of peeping, and ask, "Is this the best use of my time? Is this what I really want to be doing right now? Does this serve any good purpose?"

In the next step, you may begin to notice that, even though you know the peeping is self-defeating, you have substantial difficulty in stopping it. Try to be aware that your peeping is more than just a bad habit. Your appetite for it is more like a compulsion. Some part of you is willing to engage in negative experiences. Otherwise, you would stop this harmful peeping. See in your imagination that part of you that operates against your best interests.

Another critical peeper, a professional woman in her forties, often peeped at her seventy-year-old mother, noting with resentment how much she and her mother were alike in shyness, timidity, and difficulty in giving to themselves. Almost every time her mother bought a dress, for instance, the mother would return it a few days later with some excuse that it was not quite right.

"It is true your mother may not value herself very much," I told my client, "but in many ways she is a fine person who has had a decent life and done well by her children. However, with your peeping, which we recognize by the distress you experience, you are looking for something negative in your mother. You focus on her weaknesses to serve an unconscious agenda, and that is to resurrect and experience again your own feelings of inadequacy. In the moment you are judging your mother, you are judging yourself. You see your mother in that negative light because of your own attachment to feeling not good enough. If you can refrain from looking at her judgmentally, you will be able to see her differently and you will feel better yourself."

In summary, the critical peeper unconsciously tries to take control over the passive feeling of being himself peeped at in a critical manner. He feels peeped at, so he peeps back even more critically in return. Unfortunately, he swings back and forth between these two unpleasant ways of experiencing the world.

Appeal of Pornography

People who feast on pornography reveal problems of low self-esteem in several ways. Pornography is a visual stimulation that has a lot to do with matters other than sex, namely orality of the eyes. That refers to the unconscious willingness to feast visually on what is felt to be denied or withheld.

One man, a professional in his mid-thirties, came to see me because the fire was burning out after a year-long relationship with a pleasant and attractive woman. "Should I leave her?" he wanted to know. "What am I going to do?"

Twenty minutes into the session, my questioning had pried from him the revelation that he frequently masturbated while looking at pornography. His girlfriend, with whom he had sex about once a month, did not live with him and knew nothing of his secret activity.

"You'll never cultivate emotional intimacy with a woman with this combination of masturbation and peeping as a sideline," I told him. "When you are peeping at beautiful women in seductive poses, you are getting turned on by what you see being withheld from you. While the primary excitement for the Peeping Tom is the alleged refusal of the woman to reveal herself to him, your primary thrill is the feeling of being denied the delicious taste of the wanton woman you see exposed before you. You are like a starving man choosing to drool over the colorful illustrations in a recipe book rather than feasting on the real thing. This means you are not really interested in what is available to you, namely this girlfriend of yours who appears to have a lot to offer and who would perhaps be a good partner for you if you didn't have this emotional hang-up."

This individual had expected rejection from women and had experienced it frequently in his relationships. His parents had not been emotional or loving with each other, and he had little concept of intimacy. Because of his own low self-esteem, he was not assertive enough to communicate with this woman the meaning and significance of their relationship.

Some men with poor self-esteem like pornography because it is so safe and impersonal. There is no emotional challenge; they are not required to grow and mature. They can "love" or lust with their eyes and in their imaginations. They freeze up at the chance to show love to a real woman.

A married man might breathe heavily for hours at an X-rated movie house and then go home and ignore his wife. Or he might go home and have sex with his wife but miss out on emotional bonding with her because during sex he is only interested in romping in fantasy with the celluloid images he earlier devoured with his eyes. He teases and taunts himself with what he cannot have.

Another element in pornographic peeping is the wish to debase or to reduce women. The women are "exposed" as nothing but sex objects or "sluts." Men with this mentality are holding onto resentments against the mother-figure of their early childhoods.

"I felt devalued by Mom," goes this person's subliminal

reasoning, "now I devalue her and all women." But the alleged devaluation of this man by his mother is often nothing more than his subjective impressions of his mother's role as a foil to his infantile megalomania.

This type of man remains attached to the feelings of being devalued and rejected by women, and consequently he is blocked from achieving real closeness. As he peeps at pornography, he identifies with the one he is looking at, the one he is devaluing, and indirectly he experiences again those old feelings of worthlessness he still carries from his youth. For him, the main appeal of pornography is to "get off" on the old unresolved feelings of being humiliated, controlled, and debased.

Randall, a client in his late thirties, was annoyed that his wife resented his interest in looking at pornography and other women. He enjoyed sex movies on his VCR, *Playboy* magazines, and sexy catalogs for women's nighties and underwear.

"Now, what's wrong with that?" Randall asked. "Any red-blooded male is going to enjoy the scenery."

His wife had told him she felt inadequate and rejected by his voyeurism, and he had agreed to refrain from it. Since then, he said, he felt more compelled than ever to peep. He sneaked "porno" magazines into the house when she was out and watched sex movies on the VCR. But he had begun to feel guilty and depressed about it.

Randall's mother had been restrictive and controlling. As a teenager, he had often flirted with getting caught masturbating. He masturbated once in the living room with his grandmother sleeping close by on a sofa. He also masturbated frequently with his bedroom door open and his mother moving about the house. "I prided myself on my ability to pull it off," he grinned.

"The appeal of pornography has a lot to do with your mother and your wife, and less with naked women," I told Randall. "From what you have said today and from your previous sessions, we know you have attachments to feeling controlled, caught, punished, and humiliated. The closer you are to being caught, the more exciting it is for you. The more that certain activities are forbidden, the greater the thrill of being caught and punished.

"This unconscious part wants to flirt with these possibilities. But the more you are directed by this self-defeating side, the more you will block intimacy with your wife and suffer from your guilt and depression. The guilt is not because you are being 'naughty.' Rather, the guilt is generated because you are tangled up and indulging in feelings of being controlled by your wife, and because you are flirting with being caught and punished by her. A part of your unconscious vetoes your entanglement in these attachments, and that produces guilt. When the guilt (the feeling that you deserve to be punished) surfaces into your awareness, you attribute it to 'being naughty,' and now you become depressed about your alleged naughtiness.

"This may sound complicated," I continued. "But just focus on your growing awareness that you are secretly looking for feelings of being controlled and punished. If there is any naughtiness going on here, it is this little secret game you play with yourself, looking for control and punishment, that is so self-defeating. And notice that as you have resorted to secrecy with your magazines and movies, you are even more controlled by your wife. She may catch you in your secret activities and hold you more accountable. Even if she doesn't catch you, you are still flirting with the prospect that she will. It's all predictable: when we try to evade our issues, we make matters worse."

Like Randall's wife, women frequently slip into feeling rejected, unattractive, not good enough, even abandoned. Many women will feel this way even when their husbands or boyfriends are admiring in an acceptable way the beauty of other women. Men will always admire the beauty of women, even as they may be madly in love with one in particular.

Often the problem involves transference, meaning that a woman's issue of feeling ignored or rejected has to do with how she experienced her relationship with her own father and how she still has not worked out her attachment to the feeling of being treated or regarded in that manner.

Peepers with control issues such as Randall often enjoy sado-masochistic pornography, complete with whips, black leather boots, and scenes of domination, humiliation, and force. Here the peeper loves to identify with the "victim," and feel some of that sexual rush so sought after by sexual masochists. Even the sadist in sado-masochistic entanglements is getting his big hit off his identification with the victim, the "poor" little masochist.

Peepers of child pornography experienced in their own childhoods feelings of shame, humiliation, helplessness, and being forced to do what others wanted. Through the negative repetition compulsion, they have become either creators of the pornography, as they subject their little victims to comparable experiences and feelings, or they are the consumers of this pornography who identify with the victims in order to satisfy their unconscious attachments to those old feelings of humiliation and victimization.

Quite often everyday people produce sexual fantasies which involve scenes of domination and humiliation. Sado-masochistic fantasies are an obvious example, but often the fantasies are more subtle, such as feeling forced to perform oral sex, or feeling helpless at the mercy of an aggressive lover, or being treated scornfully by someone who is rejecting or withholding. Sometimes people feel that fantasies such as these heighten the pleasure of sex. Such fantasies are substantial evidence, if not proof, that people are able and willing to "sexualize" or libidinize certain experiences or feelings (rejection, domination, and humiliation) which would otherwise be considered negative or undesirable. Outside the realm of sex, unconscious attachments to certain negative experiences are much less obvious. When these attachments are active, there is no conscious pleasure at all—only various degrees of grief, suffering, and self-defeating behavior.

Meanwhile, sexual fantasies are the best evidence for the existence and power of the visual drive. Even the imagination of the dullest person can come alive with eye-popping color, detail, and content when his red-blooded biology goes after the pleasures of sexual make-believe.

However, the visual drive or emotional imagination is most often being engaged in a much more subtle manner. Sometimes the functioning is good, but often it is self-defeating. When we're not seeing what is unconscious, the renegade imagination gets away with stirring up negative considerations, speculations, and scenarios that attract storm clouds overhead.

Part III

Solutions and Remedies

Kindergarten in America

Before he died in 1939, Sigmund Freud pointed us in the right direction for further study and investigation. Explore the nature of self-aggression and self-defeat, he was telling us, in order to understand more precisely how and why we feel bad and wrong about ourselves and how we limit ourselves.

Freud once wrote in a footnote, "One extreme line of thought, such as the doctrine of behaviorism which originated in America, believes it possible to construct a psychology which disregards this fundamental fact (of the unconscious)."

He was aghast that Americans were establishing a system of psychology that denied the existence of consciousness. In a footnote in *Civilization and Its Discontents*, he warned that, in a culture of shallow optimism such as that of the United States, a condition may arise which he termed "the psychological misery of the masses." Ominously, a national consulting company has introduced in the past few years a Misery Index—a measure of inflation, income, debt, and taxes—that has been rising steadily.

The behavioral model Freud warned against is the cheer-leader approach to therapy. Individuals are instructed to "Just love yourself," while encouraged to employ positive affirmations, listen to canned pep-talks, and follow practical advice.

The cheerleader approach does not explain why people need all this prompting in the first place. If people need positive affirmations, they must be entrenched in negativity. From where does this negativity originate? Why do people say, "I can't do anything right," or "I have no desire to face the day," or "I feel worthless"?

In the 1930s the new science of psychology was under pressure to be more scientific. Behaviorism provided a solution, since it produces "hard facts" based on the statistical evaluation of the behavioral reactions of groups of people. But some "hard facts" are relevant and some are not. We have produced a culture of irrelevant facts, parodied by the parlor game Trivial Pursuit.

Lawrence LeShan, in *The Dilemma of Psychology*, writes that psychology "has so thoroughly sold its birthright, has so completely abandoned any real contact with human existence, that it is widely believed in our society that it would be useless to look to it for help in a time of overwhelming peril."

The behavioral model is a doctrine of rationalism. Modern man, enthralled by his rational powers, enthroned his ego as the prince of these powers. In doing so, he refuses to pay his unconscious its due respect. He certainly does not want to study (or even acknowledge) his powerful alter-ego, what psychoanalysis has called the superego, the master of the personality and the inner sanctum of our dark side.

Behaviorism is the psychology of fast answers, quick fixes, and instant results, as it tries to eradicate the symptoms while ignoring the causes. It overlooks the evolution of consciousness. It seeks to cope, not to master. It is impatient and immature, an expression of our unresolved orality.

Without deeper insight, history will continue to be framed by unconscious reactions to events. With help from the best of psychology, we can shape a future in which self-damage is contained. That means that humans must learn *to become more responsible for their unconscious reactions* as well as their conscious behaviors.

Thousands of self-defeating and self-destructive reactions spring from deep-rooted insecurities in the form of attachments to feeling inadequate, less than, and worthless. One solution is for education to undo the effects of *The Great Law,* the law that requires children to overlook or to refrain from challenging parental abuse, contradictions, lies, and other forms of emotional corruption. Already children are taught in some schools to resist being passive should any adults make sexual advances toward them.

Most people know as much about the unconscious mind and how it works as they know about brain surgery. And that's the way many people want it to stay. We are so reluctant to look at the truth of ourselves, and truth is what the unconscious is all about. Psychoanalyst Bruno Bettelheim wrote in *Freud and Man's Soul* that, though most of the bright and dedicated students he taught "were eager to learn what psychoanalysis is all about, they were largely unable to do so." Invariably, he wrote, psychoanalytic concepts became for these students "a way of looking only at others, from a safe distance—nothing that had any bearing on them." His students observed other people "through the spectacles of abstraction, tried to comprehend them by means of intellectual concepts, never turning their gaze inward to the soul of their own unconscious."

I understand this perfectly. Like everyone else, I have resisted seeing the truth of my own underlying emotional reactions. Accepting the truth about my own secret collusion in the manufacture of misery felt like taking bitter medicine. I didn't like it all. But my suffering tasted even worse.

Truth has always been a dangerous commodity, never more so than when it reveals our secret selves. H.L. Mencken once wrote, "No normal human being wants to hear the truth. It is the passion of a small and aberrant minority . . .They are hated for telling it while they live, and when they die they are swiftly forgotten . . . The man who boasts that he habitually tells the truth is simply a man with no respect for it."

Another social observer once asked, "What is the greater foolishness, the child who is afraid of the dark, or the man who is afraid of the light?"

It always felt that my parents were not interested in seeing the truth about themselves or about me. I am convinced that anything I might have said to my father that turned the spotlight on him and hinted at his dark secrets would have uncorked the rage that simmered in his breast. Once or twice I did say something powerful and direct to my mother, and she cried in self-pity and said I was cruel and selfish.

The following examples show no respect for the truth. A headline in a recent newspaper article reads, "Therapist uses common sense." This San Francisco marriage counselor tells couples, "The more you look at your problems, the lousier and more hopeless you feel."

Ignore your problems, while strengthening the rest of yourself, he recommends, adding, "Keep on the sunny side of life." According to the newspaper, people fly to him from all over the country and pay him $3,000 for a weekend workshop.

Now it has come to this, a therapist who reduces therapy to absurdity. And yet this person apparently has a big following. Well, not surprising in this orally-fixated society that people, desperate for instant answers and instant cures, rush in for his sugar pie and confirmation of their delusions.

This second item is a handout on depression given to a client of mine by her doctor who then put her on an antidepressant drug. The handout says:

"What causes depression? We do not know. We used to think it was due to something unhappy in a person's life, or to some psychological 'hang-up.' We now know, however, that this disease happens to people who have no reason to be depressed, and who have no psychiatric problems. In other words, this is a disease often affecting normal and healthy people."

Believe me, depressed people *do have* psychiatric (I prefer the word *emotional*) problems. These emotional problems are related to certain unconscious conflicts that have not been worked out and resolved. Unless a patient is in acute anxiety, incapacitated, or suicidal, the application of the right psychology will usually be better medicine than drugs. Pharmaceutical literature promoting drugs would tell you otherwise. The duplicity of that literature rivals the cigarette industry's literature on lung and throat cancers. Meanwhile, the drug industry invests huge sums of money to convince us that drug therapy is the best option for depression and everyday forms of emotional difficulty.

It is a deeper appreciation of the unconscious and its dynamics that provides the ability to see through illusions and lies. This process also roots out negativity and brings us to where we can see and maintain essential values. It means teaching higher values and unconscious operations to help each young person awaken from within.

Your value as a person is like buried treasure. The treasure is there inside you, but you have to find it.

We have to graduate from kindergarten and undertake deeper explorations of the unconscious in search of opportunities to scatter our illusions, childish fears, and self-defeating impulses.

I see the effort made every day—in the persistence, tears, and anguish of my clients, and in their delight with their own awakening—here in my office, my peephole into the great mysteries of the unconscious mind.

Hello Mommy, Hello Daddy

How necessary is it to fathom the depths of your childhood experience in order to recover from low self-esteem? And what about those adults who remember almost nothing from their early childhood and adolesence?

It is clear to me that the individuals most likely to succeed at raising self-esteem are those who begin to feel, understand, and resolve childhood feelings with parents, guardians, and siblings. Yet I have also seen people with poor memories of their past also make excellent progress by understanding themselves and their behaviors in the context of their present lives, while being able at least to imagine how they must have experienced themselves in the family of origin.

So many people say to me, "Why go into the past and bring up those old pains and hurts all over again? What's done is done, and let's get on with our lives."

In reply I tell them, "We don't look into the past in order to suffer with old feelings. Remember, your suffering in the present is a mystery we are trying to solve—and resolve.

Any good detective puts together all the clues and evidence that pertain to a case. We know from the principles of psychology that what you experienced as negative in your childhood is what you will remain emotionally attached to as an adult. You really are helping yourself when you begin to see how you transfer these unresolved negative feelings from the past onto present circumstances in your life. When you see the correlation, you are able to see that your suffering in the present is due *not* so much to the hardships of life or to the negligence of others *but* to your tendency to recreate in the present old negative feelings from the past.

"In other words, we make an 'internal adjustment' in our emotional reactions when we see and understand how we transfer hurtful feelings experienced in the past onto circumstances or people in our present lives.

"Many of us have a hard time remembering how we felt in our interactions with our parents. As children, we protected ourselves by blocking out or repressing many of those old feelings of rejection, criticism, disapproval, betrayal, and abandonment. Though the old feelings are repressed, they are not forgotten. Adults still interpret their lives and relationships through the eyes of the child part of the psyche, and then act emotionally like little children with a self-centered victim perspective. By reconnecting with those old feelings, we become aware of how we are unconsciously willing to perceive and promote those feelings in our present lives. So connecting with those feelings has the effect of deepening our awareness and insight, and making it easier for us to change for the better.

"It is illuminating and also liberating when you are able to feel how you responded to your parents, when you understand how you interpreted emotionally their behavior toward you, when you realize how you modeled yourself on their strengths and weaknesses, and when you see how in the present you are willing to hold onto old hurts and grievances. That is why we study your past. Once you really know your past, then you can put it behind you. The old feelings and negative reproaches wither and die, leaving in their place new feelings of confidence, contentment, and serenity."

To assist us in this process, we can produce an emotional inventory of those old feelings that we had with our parents and siblings. The following exercise, like others in this book, is intense and can bring up emotional feelings that have been buried for years. If strong feelings arise, that is part of the process and is not usually a cause for alarm. However, it is always best to consult a psychotherapist to help you integrate any intense emotional experiences.

Think back now on your relationship with your parents and answer the following questions. (The questions are adaptations from Nathaniel Branden's book, *Honoring The Self*. The exercise is a lot to complete at one sitting, so it may be best to read it over and work on only a few parts at a time.)

1. Did your parents allow you to express your feelings openly, or were you afraid to reveal what you thought or felt? Were you ever punished or made to feel bad for expressing these feelings?

Are you afraid as an adult to express and reveal feelings in your personal relationships? Do you feel you will be punished or seen as bad for expressing your feelings today?

2. Did your parents express their feelings with each other or with you? Or did their communications remain on a surface level?

Describe the quality of communication in your present relationships. Is it superficial or deep and intimate?

3. Did your parents listen with sincere interest to your feelings or problems, or did they make it your fault, tease you, ridicule you, or disapprove of you? Did they simply ignore your problems or dismiss them with, "I'm too busy"? Were they interested in you as a person?

Do you feel at times that your friends or family members dismiss or ignore you, or fail to listen to you with respect?

4. Did your parents support your ability to think independently, ask questions, and make your own decisions? Or were you taught to be obedient and passive, and conform to their way of doing things?

To what degree do you believe that you act independently and autonomously today?

5. Were you treated with respect? Were your feelings and ideas understood or taken seriously? Did you feel that they saw you as a unique individual, or were you invisible to them?

Are you creative in the present, or are you afraid to be expressive?

6. Did you ever have any feelings of being unwanted, a burden, or not important? Do you feel you were a source of delight for them? Did you feel loved and valued?

How much do you feel valued now by friends and family?

7. What measures did your parents use to control your behavior? Use examples, such as threats, guilt, shame, intimidation, and so on.

Explore the occurrence of guilt, shame, and intimidation in your present relationships.

8. Were your parents able to admit their mistakes and take responsibility for their behaviors? Or did they deny any wrong-doing and blame others for their faults?

Are you able to accept criticism and admit mistakes, or do you become defensive and angry?

9. Consider the extent to which you were praised and criticized by your parents? Did they put pressure on you to perform?

Do you feel you hold yourself back in the present? What blocks you from feeling more satisfied?

10. Did the interaction with your parents produce fear or guilt in you? Or a feeling of well-being? How did this work?

How would your loved ones in your present life describe the quality of their interaction with you?

Now move into this continuation of the exercise.

I. Regress back to childhood—in your imagination go back to the house you once lived in. Recall the yard and the exterior of the house. Walk in the door and see the familiar furniture. Imagine yourself as a child, somewhere between the ages of three and fifteen.

How do you feel back in the old house? Imagine your parents are there. How do you feel being back with them? Observe how you interact with both of them. What feelings are there?

II. Go over to your father. What do you want to say to him that you've never felt free to say before? What is it you are afraid to say? Tell your father what you need from him. What are the major messages that your father gave to you about life and yourself?

Can you maintain a position of strength with your parent or do you feel yourself weaken? Notice how you feel in your body?

III. Repeat the same exercise with your mother.

IV. Now write down your feelings and parental messages and how you have lived those messages out in your adult life. How do those messages still affect you today?

V. Reflect and write down ways you are just like your

father. Write down how you are like your mother. Give examples of situations where you have acted like either of your parents to others around you.

In summary, it is important to see the correlation between your past feelings with family members and the feelings you have in your present relationships. The more clearly you see this connection, (i) the more you can remain objective and detached rather than reactive, and (ii) the more you can see how a part of you remains attached to familiar but unpleasant feelings from the past.

Weeding Your Garden

Jeff came into my office one day and said he had been depressed all week.

"What's been going on?" I asked.

"Well, I'm not sure. I'm just depressed."

"Did anything significant happen this past week?'

"Can't think of anything."

"Jeff, if you're depressed, something was going on. Whatever it is, it might seem minor on the surface. But something did happen that affected you emotionally. Now we have to figure out what that was."

"Now that you mention it, my wife and I had a disagreement. It didn't seem too important at the time, but I was thinking about it on the drive here this morning, and I felt myself being angry at her." He proceeded to give me all the details of the disagreement, and ended by saying, "The more I think about it, the angrier I feel."

"Your anger is a reaction," I said. "Let's find out what precise emotional feeling has aroused your anger. Otherwise, you will feel convinced that your anger is justified by your wife's behavior, when in fact your anger is a protest to cover up your own unconscious participation in feeling bad."

After talking more about the incident, Jeff and I agreed that he had succumbed to the feeling of being overpowered and dominated by his wife's opinion, that he had felt she was forcing her views down his throat, and he had slipped passively into the feeling of being defeated by her.

"Jeff, your problem is to experience an incident such as this disagreement with your wife from the emotional perspective of control, helplessness, and defeat. As we know from your personal history, this is how you often felt with your father, that he got the best of you and required you to submit to his will. You see now that you are unconsciously willing to replay this old emotional experience with your wife. Your wife is not to blame, as your anger toward her suggests she is, although there are times when she will unwittingly play into your issue. She is just a catalyst setting off your own unconscious negative stuff.

"It is tempting to focus on the other person and make her responsible for your reactions. Instead, turn the spotlight on yourself and focus on your reactions in a situation, not on what the other person is doing or not doing."

Jeff had another problem in this example that is common to us all. He didn't know what he had been feeling on a deeper level. Initially, he was only aware of being depressed. Later, he had started to become aware of being angry toward his wife. It was very important at this point that he see beyond the anger to get to the deeper explanation for his depression. Otherwise (i) he is convinced his anger is justified by the circumstances, (ii) he holds onto his anger and suffers with it, while his wife and marriage also suffer, (iii) he is not aware of his unconscious participation in the negative experience of feeling controlled, and he will continue in the future to become entangled in those feelings and reinforce a victim mentality. He will fail to rid his garden of weeds.

Whenever you feel depressed or negative, study the following three categories to help you identify your underlying feelings. It is your attachments to these underlying feelings that result in low self-esteem. Make a note of the ones that feel familiar to you, and start to take notice of times that you slip into these feelings. These underlying or primary feelings are usually unconscious but can be accessed through your growing knowledge of how the unconscious works.

Category 1—Oral Feelings: expectations of loss; starving and going without; being held up; having to wait; being deprived of what you really want; missing out; never having enough; never feeling satisfied, feeling drained ("They take everything from me, I get nothing"); feeling refused, denied, not given to, disappointed, helpless, suffocated, devoured; watching others get away with things; seeing others excel and feeling less; feeling there is nothing here for you.

Category 2—Control Feelings: feeling taken advantage of, used, squashed, screwed, ripped off, conned, violated, tricked, lied to, persecuted, intimidated, trapped, pushed around, forced to submit, dominated, overpowered, imposed upon; having to endure inappropriate behavior; giving up your own perceptions and beliefs to others.

Category 3—Rejection Feelings: feeling abandoned, insignificant, uncared for, not wanted, excluded, looked down upon as no good, put down, criticized, unfairly accused, not understood, not liked, hated, unappreciated, dismissed, condemned, ignored, unrecognized, not taken seriously, not supported, not validated; cannot depend on anyone; feeling that you are betrayed, made a fool of, scolded, discredited, ridiculed.

These deeper feelings described above are usually covered up by (i) the surface behaviors and symptoms and (ii) the emotional reactions. Surface behaviors and symptoms include the following: compulsive eating, ambition, sex, shopping, gambling, cleaning, and other compulsions; restlessness, insomnia, no appetite, chronic fatigue; alcohol or drug abuse; impatience, compliance, self-pity, worry, sarcasm, anxiety, psychosomatic ills, pollyanna optimism, super responsible behaviors, and overwork.

The emotional reactions covering up the underlying feelings include: anger, rage, frustration, resentment, despair, sadness, fear, loss, loneliness, self-reproach; feeling inadequate, bad, stupid, guilty, shameful; blaming others; having the urge to retaliate.

This next exercise is designed to help you gain more insight into your feelings and to facilitate taking responsibility for your own emotional reactions and anxious situations.

This exercise can be used to work out any emotional reaction, altercation with others, or grievance you are holding onto with people in your past or present.

1. Describe what you perceived in the example you have chosen and define your emotional reactions. How did the situation make you feel? Go beneath the surface emotion—such as anger, fear, or sadness—and describe what you felt was done to you. For example, "I'm furious because he betrayed me; he showed no consideration for my feelings. I felt like I was nothing to him, tossed aside like an old rag doll." Or, "I felt terrified because I thought he would banish me, dump me, and leave me all alone." (For help in defining your deeper feelings, refer to the three categories described on the previous page.)

2. Take this feeling (or feelings) back into your past and describe a similar feeling in your childhood. Include childhood experiences with your parents or siblings. For example, "I remember having the same feeling with my father. One time when I washed the floor for him, he criticized me for not doing the job well enough and told me I was useless. He didn't speak to me for days." Or, "Mom always threatened to send me away to boarding school if I didn't do what she wanted." As deeply as you can, experience the feelings you had with your parent or sibling, and describe your perception of what happened and how it hurt you.

3. Go back through your life and recall how you have re-experienced those same feelings in the different contexts of your life. Are these feelings a theme in your life? For example, "Yes, I felt betrayed and not considered important in many life situations. I felt betrayed by my boss and co-workers. I felt they couldn't care less about me. It's an old feeling that I have a lot." List several of these experiences that resulted in feeling betrayed, insignificant, and not considered.

Watch for opportunities in your life where you can perceive others treating you in this manner. Do you look for it even when it is not there? Do you anticipate the feeling? Do you provoke others so that you can experience this feeling? Acknowledge the extent to which you anticipate betrayal and the degree to which you hold onto feelings of not being considered.

4. Think about what you could have done to have avoided this situation or avoided making it worse for yourself. How did you collude in bringing about the problem? For example, "I could have paid more attention to my husband and what was going on between us. I needed to communicate my feelings directly to him rather than keeping them in and

resenting him."

Even if the other person actually hurts you, your reaction to the hurt is your responsibility. You can choose to feast on the hurt or deal directly with the problem. Your perception of the situation may be totally different from the other person's. In most cases, other people do not deliberately set out to hurt you or ignore you. Once you disengage emotionally from the issue, you automatically find clarity and a more objective solution to your problem.

Are you communicating your needs and feelings directly so the other person understands you? Or are you coming at the other person in a way that causes him to feel defensive or reactive? Try not to be vague or general, such as, "I want your support." Describe exactly how he can give you the support you want.

Are you being realistic? Are you expecting that others should never say anything critical, to be there every time you have a need? If so, you are setting yourself up for disappointment.

5. Think of times when you may have betrayed others or treated them with a lack of consideration. There may be instances where you unconsciously have subjected others to the same treatment you received.

6. Describe how you treat yourself in the same manner. How do you betray yourself and treat yourself with a lack of consideration or caring?

Two Visual Meditations

Sara was a negative exhibitionist. A business manager in her thirties, she was a workaholic and a perfectionist who peeped into the faces of others for the feeling that they were looking back and seeing her as unsatisfactory in some manner.

She had never married and had linked up, in her brief and unsatisfactory relationships, with men who needed her for support or who were boring and uninteresting. In college, Sara had felt she had nothing to offer men, and had tried to "be the person that the man wanted me to be."

She would come down with a bad case of negative exhibitionism in the company of men she found attractive. Sara was convinced emotionally that "they won't find me interesting," and she then proceeded to act out her expectations by having difficulty making conversation.

"I become so concerned about what to say because I'm afraid he will find it stupid," she said. She conversed easily with certain friends, but she became tongue-tied and inarticulate when more was at stake.

Her father had been a withdrawn intellectual, and she had taken his aloofness to heart, believing it reflected inadequacies in her. She had always felt awkward trying to talk to him.

Sara was currently seeing an older man who was "safe" because he was so adoring of her. With him, however, she became a peeper instead of an exhibitionist. She peeped at him with critical eyes, looking for flaws, imperfections, and reasons she should not be with him. She saw him with the same negative appraisal with which she imagined others saw her.

Her problem extended to work where she would become mesmerized by the presence of a client facing her. "It's as if I no longer exist," she said, "and I find myself concentrating completely on the other person. I just respond to whatever the other person does or wants." In being so compliant, she was reacting to her fear of being criticized or seen as inadequate.

I recommended to her the following visual meditation. "Sara, when you stand in front of someone, you only see the other person looking back at you with what you imagine he's thinking. You're not seeing objectively. You're in a transference experience, meaning you expect to be regarded in the manner in which you felt judged and evaluated by your father. Your fear is that the other person won't like you or accept you, and so you become compliant or pleasing to try to be likeable. This is a losing strategy because you won't be respected as you fail to honor yourself or to be yourself, and you won't feel good about yourself.

"Imagine now that you're standing in front of some person, and that instead of seeing him *with* your eyes you are seeing him *through* your eyes. This is hard to explain. You will grasp it better experientially, which means you must feel your way into this new way of seeing. You would be seeing, not the sight of him looking critically at you, but an impression of him just standing there waiting for you to do a little dance with him, one which you are capable of leading, one in which you are intent on your own satisfaction. You would be seeing him with no judgment, no preconceived notions, simply looking for whatever you can see that pleases and amuses you. You do not judge him and you do not care whether or how he judges you.

"Now, imagine that he is not seeing you personally, but rather just a figure standing in front of him. You can imagine you have become a composite of all people—you are now every man and every woman. Imagine that his gaze goes through you and comes out the other side, and that he doesn't even know who or what you are—but that he only sees what he imagines you represent.

"In this meditation, feel yourself in your own body, be aware of your breathing, feel yourself grounded and strong in your legs. Imagine the pure essence of yourself in your heart and mind, looking out at this person from *behind* your eyes, not *with* your eyes. You want nothing and you need nothing from this person. But you are open to whatever possibilities can be created through the encounter. Feel how you are creating an experience of your own self emerging from dungeons deep in the underground of your psyche to see the world in a whole new way."

Another shy client, Mark, did not know the difference between positive exhibiting and negative exhibiting. At meetings of fellow professionals, for instance, he would begin to express himself in an impressive manner (positive exhibiting), recommending to the group some sensible course of action and giving his reasons.

The moment he was challenged, however, he took it personally and began to get tangled up in feeling criticized and belittled. He immediately felt he should not have said anything, that he had said it wrong, that he had made a fool of himself, that it was better to keep quiet. Now he reverted to silence, convinced that his presentation had been inappropriate and that he was being peeped at for his inappropriateness.

The root of the problem was Mark's secret attachments to criticism and disapproval. Even in situations where criticism was not implied, he would look for criticism because of the unconscious part of himself that was attached to that feeling.

Now he would defend, "I'm not looking for criticism, the problem is I said it wrong. I shouldn't have said it and now I'm going to keep my mouth shut."

The following exercise illustrates how the emotional imagination can be used to help a person expand beyond self-centeredness and insecurities, and develop more objectivity.

Suppose you are having a conflict with another person, and you feel that this person believes you are inferior or unworthy. The more you focus on the other person's alleged perspective of you, the more likely you will fail to see the self-defeating element in yourself.

Make yourself comfortable, breathe fully in a relaxed fashion, close your eyes and imagine that you are now becoming the person who you believe sees you as inferior. Try to feel what this person is feeling. Try to see the world through the eyes of this person. In other words, feel what it is like to be this person.

As you continue this perspective, imagine that this person sees you walk into a room. See yourself through the eyes of your antagonist. Be conscious of whatever feelings arise. Continue to watch yourself through this other person's eyes. If this person has a negative impression of you, can you not feel that may be a result of this person's own problems or issues that have nothing to do with you?

If you can sense that he is indeed looking at you as an inferior, then you will be able to sense that he must be judgmental and negative himself to regard you in such a light. It may be that this person makes a negative judgment of you because he sees in you (or believes he sees in you) some negative trait he is unwilling to see in himself. Therefore, he is not seeing you objectively. So you don't have to be upset by his impression of you. And if you are, it's because your unconscious wants to use this situation to indulge in the sense of your inadequacy or worthlessness.

Many people have a difficult time with this exercise. First, they dislike the feeling of leaving their own self-centered way of looking at things. Second, they are secretly attached to feeling a victim of the other person's impressions, and they do not want to let go of this feeling by getting a new perspective. Third, it feels alien to see themselves as others see them, especially through the eyes of what is felt to be an antagonist.

You might be able to feel your antagonist looking at you with regrets for the separation between you both, and maybe he is struggling for understanding, too, and would like to generate better feelings toward you.

Creative Blocking

Thinking has a visual component, for productive thoughts are often flashes of in-*sight*. While hunger is a signal to take in food, the signal to begin thinking is the anxiety caused by the difficulty or failure to understand or comprehend something.

This anxiety or even inner fear that triggers the thinking process is a repeat of the infantile situation in which much of life was both fearful and not understood. To quell the fear, some product of thinking (an explanation) is required. Much of the time the explanation is far from the truth or the facts, but that is incidental. Some explanation, however improbable, can serve to quell the fear. For example, the myth of Adam and Eve provides an explanation for our existence, without which some people would feel very alone in the dark.

Much mental energy is used up by the production of rationalizations and compensations for inner conflicts, passivity, and attachments to our grievances. Little energy may be left over for more productive or fulfilling thinking.

Through thinking processes, people develop their own brands of beliefs, prejudices, and opinions. Whenever these are challenged, especially by the truth, a negative emotional reaction such as denial, fear, or indignation is predictable.

The hero's journey involves exploring these emotional reactions to see and understand what is blocking him from the truth about himself, from being creative, and feeling fulfilled. It is fearfulness in facing his inner self that keeps him from being at peace with himself.

As mentioned, a great deal of so-called objective thinking serves emotional aims. For instance, a cynical observer of the world scene may be seeing correctly the futility of certain social or political actions. But the degree to which he is emotionally burdened by his unconscious attachments to disappointment and loss blocks him from producing constructive solutions or alternatives that might guide others.

Rachel, a professional in her mid-30s, was imbued with the emotional conviction of her inadequacy. She said she felt "intellectually paralyzed by anxiety, like I'm constantly in a fog." She had much difficulty seeing or thinking of positive outcomes, and she had not set any goals nor imagined where she might go with her career. Rachel's mental functioning became most active only when she was focused on something she was worried about.

"I'm always thinking what's going to go wrong if I do this, or do that," she said. "I can even be anxious about polishing my shoes. When will I do them? Will I put too much polish on them? Will I get the polish on my hose or fingernails? Then I'll start to think about shoes in general, that I need another pair, but will I find my size, and when will I get to the mall, and I can't go because my room's a mess and I have to clean it, and I have to write a letter tonight, but I better get to sleep early or I'll be exhausted at work, and when will I see my boyfriend, and I'll start to worry about that relationship.

"My thinking just goes on and on like that," Rachel lamented. "It keeps me in a state where I've no way in hell of knowing what's going on, really. I'm stressed out, and everything is confused and jumbled. I'm confused and jumbled. I feel that everything's like a jigsaw puzzle I have no hope of figuring out."

Rachel had a visual block based on some resistance to (or fear of) seeing things clearly. She noted that on the job, for instance, her co-workers observed important details that she completely missed. She remembered "not wanting to see or consider the nasty things a friend was saying about me." As a little girl, she had been fearful of people and reluctant to go to birthday parties and elementary school. Her mother often kept her home from school at the slightest sign of physical discomfort.

"What was painful for you in thinking or seeing certain things?" I asked her. She replied without hesitation, "It was to look at people, at the world. I was so scared of it. It was better not to look."

Like a shy person who, as a child, decides not to speak for fear of revealing the "forbidden" something he has seen, Rachel made a choice not to think or see for fear of uncovering more lurking dangers and forbidden byways in the scary world around her. As a child, she had absorbed and then repressed much of her mother's fear. The mother was a borderline phobic obsessed with locking doors "to keep out dangerous people." Often Rachel's father was away overnight, and she had to accept her frightened mother as her only protector. In Rachel's mind, death and annihilation awaited her in any encounter with a "dangerous" person. As an adolescent, she had had a serious operation and had confronted the prospects of her death.

She made this inner arrangement to cope with her fear of annihilation: "Whatever I agree to think or see will only be for the sole purpose of avoiding problems or danger." As an adult, much of her emotional imagination was absorbed with futile and worrisome speculations about her immediate future, leaving her in a state of constant anxiety and draining her creative energy.

She was constantly afraid of being wrong and, consequently, had great trouble making decisions. Whenever she made a decision, her inner voice was very likely to "second-guess" her and to assail her with doubt and criticism. "I feel crucified by my inner voice," she said. "Whichever way I decide on an issue, I know I'm going to get it." So she felt safer remaining immobilized and inactive.

Rachel also had no vision of future prosperity. Once in the company of her boyfriend, she spotted a new luxury car and said, "What a lovely car, but I'll never have anything like that." When something desirable popped into her mind, such as a house in a rich neighborhood or a high-paying job, she said, "I quickly block it out and the impression just fades away. I say to myself: 'Oh, give me a break, I'll never have anything like that. Don't think about it because it's not going to happen.'"

As she became aware of these unconscious blocks, and worked out her repressed fears, her emotional imagination came to life in a positive manner and she began to feel more fulfilled and to see a future that was adventuresome rather than scary.

Rachel had finally freed herself from obsessional thinking, those worrisome, extraneous speculations that once plagued her. In general, obsessional thinking is the result of an individual's secret affinity for feeling helpless and out of control. The defense goes like this, "I am not passively attached to feeling helpless in my life (or in this situation);

Look at how active my mind is in trying to solve these problems and sort things out." Like most psychological defenses, this is self-defeating. The more a person obsesses, the more likely he feels overwhelmed and ineffective.

Here is an exercise that individuals can do on their own in order to gain more understanding of the roots of their fears.

1. To begin to flush fear out of your system, sit down and write everything you have a fear of. For example, "I'm afraid my wife might leave me" or "I'm afraid of getting old" or "I'm afraid of being poor and homeless."

2. Once you have listed the fears, now begin to focus on each one. For each one, ask yourself, "What am I afraid of?" For example, let us say you have listed fear of driving. Write out the feelings that come up as you imagine yourself driving. Be honest with yourself. As you imagine yourself driving, describe your worst-case scenario. Example, "I get in the car, go down the road, lose control, the car crashes, and I am killed."

3. Pursue the image. Ask yourself, what is the worst thing that could happen? Example, "Oh, my family will be so upset, and I won't have to go to work anymore." This statement suggests an individual is thinking about crashing and dying because he wants to get out of doing something or facing something in his life. Ask yourself, how and in what way do you have such feelings in the context of your life? Someone feeling trapped and dissatisfied with life could indeed produce fantasies or feelings of being in an accident and dying.

4. What have you learned about yourself from this exercise? Have you identified some conflict, problem, or dissatisfaction in your life that your fear or phobia may represent symbolically or metaphorically? To cure your fear,

you now have to begin to find some way to resolve the underlying conflict and also to become aware of the degree to which your emotional imagination is used against yourself.

Remember one thing—fear can serve as the best possible excuse for maintaining your passivity and keeping you mired in low self-esteem. Fear along with denial and blaming represent resistance to personal growth.

Emotional blocks can be a major impediment to creativity and progress. Some scientists with voyeuristic inhibitions work for decades in their fields without producing or publishing anything new. But when someone else comes out with a new idea, they will ignore, reject, or attack it.

The British almost overlooked Darwin's theory of evolution. The famous paper on the subject was read to the Linnaean Society of London in 1858. The society's president then ignored it. In his report for the year, the president regretted that 1858 had "not been marked by any of those striking discoveries which at once revolutionize, so to speak, the department of science on which they bear."

The public reacted enthusiastically when Darwin published his book *Origin of The Species* in 1859. The book was sold out on the day of publication and raised emotional reactions that continue today.*

Sometimes creativity is blocked because individuals are afraid to be wrong, and so they do nothing that is innovative. If they were perceived to have done it wrong, they would expect to be judged as stupid, incompetent, unworthy. The prospect of this creates fear, which is a consequence of their attachments to feeling inadequate and unworthy. So they cope with their fear by conforming to orthodoxy, playing it safe.

* *This example was cited by Edmund Bergler in "Curable and Incurable Neurotics"*

Limits Of Our Vision

It had been a memorable summer day. My wife Sandra, our son Matthew, and I had climbed up to Paradise Point on a five-mile hike on the slopes of Mount Rainier. We were on vacation in Washington state, and after the climb we had a late lunch at Paradise Inn and began a two-hour drive into Seattle.

En route we turned at a town junction, and suddenly saw somebody fall out the passenger door of a pickup truck and tumble onto the road less than 100 feet ahead. A small white Ford directly in front of us ran right over this person. In the instant before the car hit, I saw his face clearly, a teenage boy framed in fear and anguish. We three groaned in dismay as we saw the car's left wheels thumping into his body.

The car bounced over the boy's thighs and swerved off to the side of the road ahead. I pulled off the pavement across from him. We saw that he was conscious, turning his head to look around, then trying to raise himself on his elbows. I dashed out of my car to him, and the driver from the truck got to him first. The man picked him up and carried him off the road.

The boy moaned and said he was alright. I imagined that, at least, his legs were broken, and I was relieved when the man put him down before more damage was done to his body. Lying there beside the road, he tried to get up. I put my hands on him, urging him to lie still.

The boy insisted, "I'm okay, I want to get up, I'm okay." But he didn't look okay; he seemed to be drowning in pain. Then he began to murmur, "I want to die, I want to die."

"Don't talk like that, don't talk like that!" said the man, apparently his father. "I told you before about closing that door properly."

I realized this man had not seen the boy run over because he indicated he thought the boy had fallen under the wheels of his own truck. But the driver of the white car was now among us, a woman stunned and profusely apologetic, and the father finally understood what had happened.

The boy was getting to his feet and we helped him. He wobbled but was able to support his own weight. He kept repeating this wish to die, and I realized his pain was perhaps more emotional than physical. The boy refused his father's suggestion that he be taken immediately to a medical clinic.

"No," he insisted, he just wanted to die, and he repeated it several times. That was all he wanted, and he was so emphatic about it.

With help from us, he hobbled over and sat in the truck on the seat from where he had fallen. There he wept and was consoled by his father. His crying was so pitiful, and his continued wish to die so earnest, that I soon felt myself pushed back across the road to my car, retreating from this pain that was worse than broken bones, something like lost hope, shattered dreams, and ultimate despair.

This had not been an accident, I decided. Accidents are rare when we are alert and aligned with the precious quality of life. Unconsciously, and perhaps even consciously, in some moment of grave disharmony with his father and within himself, the boy had precipitated this event.

In my mind as I drove along I told the boy: "Don't stop believing in yourself. Trust that you have some special purpose for your life, some wonderful destiny. You can be the hero and not the victim in the great drama of your life. Take on that challenge, go ahead and do it, and your life will have direction and meaning. If you want that kind of life, there will be opportunities and helpers to set the stage for you."

There are ways of seeing the mystery of our pain, and there are pathways I know of that lead to freedom from it. On the continuing drive into Seattle, I resolved to teach more people what I knew about self-suffering.

As parents and teachers, we have to know what our children are feeling, and help them to express themselves, teach them to speak for the self within, and give them that liberty, even if we did not have it ourselves.

Our self-centeredness would have us believe that if our children look okay to us on the surface, or if they are coping, than there is nothing more to see or understand. We choose not to see beneath the surface of ourselves and those closest to us.

Parents who are ignorant or narcissistic fail to recognize and appreciate a child in his own right. Often they take a child for granted, as if the child is little more than an extension of their own selves. These parents usually did not get recognition from their own parents, and so they have little sense of what they are failing to pass on to their own children. Presence, not presents, is what a child loves most. This means that he feels the parent's full recognition of him and that the parent respects and honors him in his own right. The parent who does this is conscious of the value of his child and this consciousness is seen and felt by the child. This is a great help for the child in appreciating his own value.

Young people may be having a harder time than we realize because the prevailing mentality seems to be stripped of essential values. The hardships for the young are not only what they do see of neglect and indifference that torments them but also what they do not see. They are prisoners of the limits of their vision, our vision.

American Indians, who had this land before us, saw all created things as sacred. The Great Spirit was seen in the wind, the trees, grass, rivers, mountains, and animals. Indians saw that all aspects of nature, like man himself, partook of this divinity.

Even as modern civilization made us more dependent on our eyes, we became blind. We do not see the sacred; we are enthralled with our self-importance; and we identify with our egos instead of with the whole of creation.

William Blake, the great English poet, conveyed this understanding when he wrote 200 years ago, "This life's dim windows of the soul, Distort the heavens from pole to pole, And leads you to believe a lie, When you see with, not through, the eye."

If we cannot see sacredness in nature, we will not see it in the children. We will not fathom the meaning and significance of our humanity, and we will be the weak link between the past and the future.

We are not even seeing a bright future for the children. In the last several years, I have probably seen a dozen movies depicting conditions in America one or more decades into the future. Every one of these movies depicts more violence, poverty, pollution, and anarchy. Are these dismal imaginings not extensions of our present course? The movies show plenty of technological advances but not an inkling of the possibility of emotional or psychological development. If this is what we imagine, surely this is what we shall create.

This negative projection mirrors the attitude of many of my new clients, everyday professional and working people who are struggling with emotional hang-ups and low self-esteem. "You mean there's hope for me!" they exclaim in their first session. "Are you saying that this will work, that happiness is a real possibility!" What underlies these remarks but degrees of hopelessness and quiet despair. What is the vision of people in this state of mind? Go see *Blade Runner, The Running Man, Terminator 2, Freejack, Total Recall,* or *Escape From New York.*

Peace and love in 2025 can be creative, fulfilling, and exciting in ways our minds have yet to dream of. As we focus our emotional imagination, we can begin to see the harmonious country we want our children to inherit, and we can turn and travel in that direction.

Our lack of vision is also apparent to poor and minority children. They can see and feel that they are not valued. These youngsters have been abandoned by the ruling class in America, unloved by the white majority, given up as if they could not possibly have anything to offer. The consequences are apparent in the inner cities. These children are *our* children, and we will all suffer if they are not given a chance to have a good life. It is not enough to say that anyone who is strong enough and smart enough can pull himself up by the bootstraps. This is used as a rationale for the self-centered individual whose constricted vision sees only as far as his immediate family's prosperity. It may be that our greatest problem as a nation resides in how we fail to value each other.

Indian nations had the vision quest to help young people find their way. Indians went out alone onto the plains or into the woods and remained in solitude for several days in the cold and darkness, sometimes without food or water.

The ordeal was intended to produce a vision that provided a young person with a sense of purpose or mission in life. Even if his vision were vague, and even if the youngster had none at all, he was still imbued in the ritual with the sense of the mystery and wonder of life and inspired to find his unique place in it.

In my vision quest, I see a country that emphasizes the value of education and creativity and which teaches children to be themselves, to value themselves, to express themselves, to be original, genuine, unique. This society fosters creative arts, nature appreciation, environmental protection and enhancement, and mastery of skills and of self. In this future, wisdom, personal excellence, and cooperation are valued attainments.

This future society gets its strength and integrity by promoting the sovereignty and independent value of each of its members. Instead of controlling or dictating values and morality, which prompts rebellion, the new way inspires cooperation by teaching each person how important he or she is to the well-being and prosperity of all. Crime, violence, prejudice, and selfishness will be on the wane as each person is taught to champion the values of compassion, integrity, dignity, and justice.

This is not being unrealistic or hopelessly idealistic. It is a plan, a vision, a purpose. The knowledge is available. We only have to be inspired to move this dream along.

Not long ago my son asked me, "Do you know what you are supposed to do in your life?"

I answered that I hoped to contribute something to the improvement of society, to help people understand themselves better for the promotion of peace and happiness. I added, "I have to be careful that I'm not doing something that is good but for the wrong reasons, or I will probably fail. I have to keep looking inside to see where I'm coming from."

"That's a decent mission you're on," he said. "I hope I find mine too."

I let it go at that. I did not want to offer anything so mundane as advice when he was contemplating his destiny. I was just glad he was entertaining notions of a noble purpose and rich adventure for his life.

To the visions of our future, let me add, may the powers of creation intervene on behalf of the boy who wanted to die, and may my generation leave a rich legacy of psychological insight for the ones to come.

More Remedies

As I have been saying, the most powerful remedy for low self-esteem is *insight*. With insight, you are able to identify the exact self-defeating feelings, thoughts, and visual processes that sabotage feeling good about yourself.

Once you identify your negative attitudes and how you use your emotional imagination to "see" deprivation, rejection, and failure, you gradually find confidence returning.

In other words, if you want to boost your self-esteem, you have to dismantle the way you are perceiving yourself, others, and the circumstances in your life. Low self-esteem is a result of seeing yourself and your interactions with others "incorrectly." These faulty perceptions derive from unresolved childhood perceptions, hurts, and grievances that are transferred onto others or events in your present life.

Insight is much more than a mental process. It involves the discovery of unpleasant emotions that have been repressed since childhood. These include rejection, betrayal, criticism, disapproval, and other negative emotions that you felt as a child, and which remain obstacles to your peace and happiness unless they are acknowledged and worked out. The process involves your ability to reconnect with those old feelings, as well as to understand your unconscious willingness to promote and experience those feelings in the present. Many of the exercises in this book, as well as the case histories, can help readers make that connection with their repressed feelings.

Once you cease to anticipate negative experiences and negative reactions, you automatically feel better about yourself. Your esteem improves as you see your emotional involvement in resisting change and holding on to grudges and hurts. You become aware of how you indulge unconsciously in feeling deprived, controlled, criticized, rejected, and you see the power and effect of your self-aggression and how it instigates self-reproach and even self-hatred.

Once you see what you are holding onto, you have the choice to let it go. When people do not see their attachments, they are not aware they are holding onto something that results in misery and self-defeat.

The following remedies and exercises are designed to help you identify the problem and to begin the process of deepening your insight into your emotional reactions. The exercises will help you gain insight—but are not a cure-all. They are best applied in conjunction with psychotherapy.

Gathering Insight

This exercise is intended to provide more insight into your self-depreciating beliefs—why you do not like yourself, why you do not believe in yourself, and why you hold yourself back. To raise self-esteem, you begin by developing an inventory of relevant information about your past and present.

1. List and describe your positive characteristics and attributes.
2. List and describe your major weaknesses and limitations. What are you rejecting in yourself?
3. What would you like to change in yourself? What inner qualities would you like to manifest in your life? What are the excuses you give yourself to explain why you have not yet succeeded?
4. How would you like your life to be? What are your positive scenarios?
5. What are the negative scenarios for yourself that you see in your future?
6. List your five biggest fears. Explain why you fear these things. What is the worst thing that could happen?
7. I'm angry because . . . (complete)
8. I'm tired of . . . (complete)
9. I want . . . (complete)
10. How would you describe yourself from a mental or intellectual point of view?
11. How would you describe yourself from an emotional or feeling point of view?
12. How would you describe yourself physically? What do you like about your body? Dislike? How would you like your body to be? What can you do to establish a better and more pleasurable relationship with your body?
13. Describe the major successes in your life. What contributed to your success?
14. Describe and list your failures? Why did you fail?
15. Describe a situation(s) where you really felt good about yourself. What feelings were present? How did you feel toward others and the world? How does it feel inside to recall these memories?
16. Compose a vision of where you would like to be in five years, from a external or material standpoint as well as

an inner development standpoint.

Parental Images

It is very helpful to develop the capacity to feel the emotional hardships you felt as a child. This is done not to suffer in the present moment, of course, but in order to understand more deeply the precise feelings that remain unresolved from your past. Answer the following questions with whatever comes to you without too much thinking. When finished, answer the same questions substituting your father.

1. What kind of person was your mother?
2. How would you describe your relationship with her?
3. What was your mother's favorite saying about life?
4. How did your mother praise you—what did she say?
5. How did your mother criticize you—what did she say?
6. When mother was upset, how did she show it?
7. How did you respond when she was upset?
8. What were her expectations of you? How did she hope you would turn out?
9. What did your mother like most about you?
10. What did she dislike most about you?
11. How do you wish your mother might have been different?
12. What would you like from your mother? What did you need from her?
13. Be your mother right now. As your mother, how would you describe the son or daughter you are? Have her talk about the kind of relationship she had with you.
14. Make a list of all the strengths or positive qualities you see in your mother. Note how these are reflected in yourself, either through manifesting them now or because you have rebelled aginst them and cultivated the opposite

qualities. Try to be objective in seeing both your mother's strengths and your own.

15. Write a list of your mother's major weaknesses. Note how these are reflected in yourself, through acceptance or rejection of the traits. Be specific.

16. Write down the limitations in your life that you carry from your mother. How are you similar? Describe the pain and problems that are created for you by these limitations.

17. Make a statement that you would like to say to your mother, a statement that you feel nervous about making, but which summarizes what you have always wanted to say.

Keep in mind, you will be most similar in personality and temperment to the parent with whom you had the most difficulty.

Self-Imposed Put-Downs

Read each positive statement and reflect on it. Before going to the next statement, jot down as honestly as you can any negative comments that come to you.

1. I am very pleased with myself.
2. I am a total success.
3. I always get what I want.
4. I have always been approved of and well-liked by others.
5. I never worry about winning the approval of or pleasing others.
6. I trust my ideas, perceptions, and opinions explicitly.
7. I have no difficulty making decisions and following through on them.
8. I only attract loving, positive people in my life.
9. I am happy with myself, even if the opposite sex is not present.
10. I feel confident in expressing my feelings and having

them acknowledged.

11. The expression of my intelligence and creativity helps and uplifts others.

It is likely that you often reproach yourself with the negative comments you have composed in this exercise. As long as you believe these reproaches, you will miss out on happiness, success, and fulfillment. You hold onto these beliefs to ensure that you will continue to feel deprived, cheated, rejected, and controlled. Your addiction is to loss and deprivation, and you justify the loss by claiming to be inadequate.

Career Set Points

Many people have *set points* which limit how much money they feel they can earn. Unconsciously, we don't allow ourselves to earn more than what our *set point* has established. We don't see or visualize ourselves making more. Many relatively successful business people have this problem.

Imagine yourself making double your present income.Visualize yourself in some realistic situation in which this doubling is feasible. What feelings does it bring up for you to see yourself making more money? Do you feel you don't deserve to make more? Perhaps you would feel guilty about having "too much." Maybe you feel you will be drained in the effort (the feeling of being drained is usually an emotional problem). Can you sense how you may be comfortable earning less, when you could be making a lot more with only a little more effort?

Now take a moment and picture yourself as vividly as possible having a powerful will that sends you marching along life's path with a firm and decided step. See yourself acting in various situations with focus, concentration, purpose, and sense of direction. See yourself attaining all that you can imagine is within your reach. In choosing to be yourself, what feelings does that bring up for you?

Repeat this process to learn more about what may be holding you back from moving into a higher level of skill or professionalism in your career.

Remember that fear and anxiety can be excuses to justify your passivity. Anxiety can result because you are really more comfortable with feelings of missing out, not getting, being deprived. Or your anxiety may relate to irrational feelings that the requirements of success will overwhelm you.

Unblocking Creativity

Make a list of all the demands that you place on yourself. What do you want with respect to relationships, career, friends, and community? What do you want to achieve with respect to your personal self, i.e. happiness, peace of mind, emotional strength?

A. Now read the list and write *I should* in front of every statement. How does this feel? Do you recognize anyone you know as the voice of "I should?"

B. Now put *I can't* in front of each statement and give excuses for each one. What does this bring up for you? Are your excuses realistic or based on fear and guilt?

C. Now put *I don't want to* in front of each statement. How does this feel? Saying this makes us more aware of the power of our resistance. Realize that *should* and *can't* are soft ways of saying, "I really don't want to."

D. Now write *I'm afraid to because* . . . for each statement. Try to locate the origins of your fears from childhood.

E. Now redo the list and write *I will* in front of each statement. How does this feel?

Whenever we say, I should *or* I can't *or* I'm afraid, *we convince ourselves to believe we are less capable than we really are. Remember, it is our willingness to be responsible for whatever we feel and do that brings a sense of power and capability.*

See Yourself Succeeding

When you are self-conscious or shy, you look out on the world from your own self-absorption to observe how you are being seen by others.

Imagine that you could see yourself from some other perspective. There is another way and it is very effective in reducing anxiety associated with fears of rejection, criticism, and disapproval. It is especially effective for someone nervous about speaking in front of others.

If you are scheduled to talk to a group, it is likely your most prevalent visualizations of yourself performing the task involve you standing up or sitting before the group and, through your eyes, seeing their faces looking back at you.

Try this instead. Imagine that you become a witness to yourself. When you begin to worry and to peep and to see yourself doing badly with your speech, use your imagination to put your eyes in that witness part of you that stands like a ghost or a guardian angel at the back of the room or off to the side. Now, from that vantage, you see yourself up there in front of the group, talking to the group.

You will be able to feel that this witness part is aligned with your best interests, as if he or she represents the best in you. From his vantage point, you can begin to feel that it is easier to imagine yourself doing well. You might even observe yourself being superb with your presentation, better than you ever thought you could. This is how you can expand beyond what you thought yourself capable of.

The fact that, in this visualization, you are *not* looking into the faces of the audience helps you feel calmer, more composed, more sure of yourself. From this perspective, it is easier to generate confidence as you see yourself succeeding. Every time you become anxious about your impending speech, switch your imagination into this mode and see yourself from the witness position. If you persist in doing this, you will be pleasantly surprised. The technique will generate confidence about yourself and your abilities that will carry you forward with more self-assurance when it is time to actually face the audience.

This exercise can also be done to see yourself succeeding in a variety of challenging situations.

This technique is effective because it gets you out of your self-centeredness where you are trapped in your emotional limitations and enables you to see with more objectivity.

Inner-Child Reunion

Read through this exercise and then close your eyes and imagine it happening. Or you can have a friend read the exercise to you, but make sure the pace is slow enough. Plan to take ten to fifteen minutes.

Relax and be conscious of your breathing. Observe any tension in your body, in your mind, and continue to follow your breathing until you succeed, at least somewhat, in relaxing.

In your imagination go to your favorite place—a quiet spot or special haven—perhaps one you remember from childhood. Imagine walking to this place. Take your time in getting there. If you can, notice aspects or details of the walk. Now you arrive at your special haven, and you see standing or sitting there in the center a child who is the child you were. He or she can be an age from three to fifteen.

How does the child look? Notice his or her emotional state.

Imagine your child looks up and sees you, your adult

self. How does your child react? What feelings or needs does he or she express?

Go over to your child and relate to him or her. Ask what your child needs. Listen to your child speak to you. Allow your child to say whatever he or she wants to say. If your child is hesitant to talk, just imagine what your child wants to say.

Respond back to your child. Tell your child what you are feeling.

Take your child in your arms. What are you feeling as you do so? What does your child represent for you?

Tell your child you will always be there for him or her. Hear what your child has to say in return.

Part company with your child and come back to your present situation. Jot down your impressions of the exercise and any words that convey your emotional state.

Self-Esteem Creed

---

1. I am responsible, not others, for how my life has turned out. There is no one else to blame for my decisions, indecisions, or my own negative feelings.

2. I do not need the permission of others, nor their encouragement, to do what I feel is best for me or to pursue my aspirations. I do not need to be validated by some outside source.

3. I am free to be myself and express who I am. I accept myself as I am right now. I am not concerned with whether or not other people approve or disapprove of who I am and what I believe in. Feeling good about myself does not depend on the actions or responses of others.

4. I do not depend on others to make decisions for me nor to indicate to me whether I am doing the right or wrong things.

5. I do not need to prove to anyone my worth and importance.

6. I do not take slights, disagreements, or differences with others as an indication that they do not like me or are against me.

7. I do not blow the normal frictions of everyday life into major catastrophes.

8. I do not look for opportunities to feel rejected, criticized, ignored, or dismissed in my relationships or the circumstances of my life.

9. I am able to be objective about myself and admit my mistakes. I regard making personal mistakes as a natural part of my growth process.

10. I do not beat myself up with guilt over mistakes I committed in my past, nor do I reproach myself for being inadequate, undesirable, or not good enough.

11. I do not waste my energy judging others, feeding off their faults or being critical of their choice to be, think, or feel the way they do.

12. I do not need to be perfect to feel good about myself.

13. I am not afraid to express my value judgments and to stand up for what I believe, even when others may denounce my opinions.

14. I do not hesitate to express my loving feelings to others.

15. I trust in other peoples' capacity to take care of themselves, make their own decisions and handle their own life issues.

16. I do not live for the purpose of satisfying other peoples' needs or to make them happy. Nor do other people exist to satisfy my needs or make me happy.

17. I respect my inner signals, the voice of my authentic self, even though they may not conform to conventional morality or the prevailing viewpoint. I am not afraid to act on those inner signals.

Bibliography

Bergler, Edmund. *Curable and Incurable Neurotics.* Liveright, New York, 1961. (The 181-page chapter in this book entitled "The Visual Drive" was a major source of understanding and inspiration for my book.)

Bergler, Edmund. *Tensions Can Be Reduced to Nuisances.* Liveright Publishing Co., New York, 1978.

Bergler, Edmund. *The Writer and Psychoanalysis.* International Universities Press. Madison, CT. (First published by Doubleday & Co. 1950, 1951).

Bettelheim, Bruno. *Freud's Vienna & Other Essays,* Vintage Books, New York, 1991.

Branden, Nathaniel. *Honoring The Self: Personal Integrity and the Heroic Potentials of Human Nature.* Jeremy Tarcher Inc., Los Angeles, 1983.

Brown, Joseph Epes. *The Spiritual Legacy of the American Indian.* Crossroad Publishing, New York, 1987.

Diagnostic And Statistical Manual of Mental Disorders (Third Edition—Revised). American Psychiatric Association, Washington, D.C. 1987.

Franck, Frederick. *The Zen of Seeing.* Vintage Books, New York, 1973.

Gay, Peter. *Freud: A Life for Our Time.* W. W. Norton & Co., New York, 1988.

Gay, Peter, Ed. *The Freud Reader.* W. W. Norton & Co., New York, 1989.

LeShan, Lawrence. *The Dilemma of Psychology.* Dutton, New York, 1990.

Selected Papers of Edmund Bergler, M.D. (1933-1961). Grune and Stratton, New York, 1969.

About the Author

Peter Michaelson is a psychotherapist in private practice. Before becoming a psychotherapist, he worked as a professional journalist, and for several years he specialized in reporting on science and health subjects for a national news agency. Mr. Michaelson gives seminars on raising self-esteem and on overcoming the emotional problems of addictive personalities. For the past several years, he has trained other psychotherapists in his clinical methods. He has recently moved to Santa Fe, NM.

More titles from Prospect Books

The Emotional Catering Service: The Quest for Emotional Independence, by Sandra Michaelson. 264 pages. Quality paperback. $15.95.

"The essence of emotional independence comes in our struggle to discover the truth of ourselves, not in getting others to change."

From *The Emotional Catering Service*

Do You:

• Compulsively seek approval, compare yourself to others, and find it difficult to receive recognition?

• Take responsibility for others, sacrifice yourself to serve their needs, and take the blame for everything that goes wrong?

• Deny your own needs, limit yourself, and feel unappreciated in your relationships?

• Fear confrontations, go along with the agendas of others, and allow them to direct your thoughts and feelings?

If you resonate with these feelings and behaviors, you are running an Emotional Catering Service. If you want to close up shop, this book's innovative approach offers you transforming insights and techniques to liberate you from this powerful emotional addiction.

You will learn:

How to appreciate yourself for who you are rather than for what you do • How not to take things personally • How to dissipate feelings of anger, dissatisfaction, and despair • New ways to develop intimacy and express love without fear of rejection • How to assert yourself when appropriate, think independently, and express your rights and feelings without fear • The ability to define clearly what you want and live by your own inner voice.

Sandra Michaelson is a psychotherapist and lecturer who has developed a new, in-depth approach to therapy that cures people of emotional distress and self-defeating behaviors.

Also from **Prospect Books:**

Secret Attachments: Exposing the Roots of Addictions and Compulsions. by Peter Michaelson. 208 pages. Quality paperback. $14.95.

To order, send **$14.95** plus $4 shipping and handling to:

Prospect Books, P.O. Box 8362
Santa Fe, N.M. 87501
Or call direct 1-800-444-2524

Excerpt from *Secret Attachments:*

That we all have a negative side of ourselves is readily apparent. The opposing human conditions of truth and falsehood, courage and cowardice, good and evil, have been expressed dramatically in mythology, religion, and literature since the dawn of humanity. Men and women cannot escape participation in the battle between these antagonistic forces. The struggle for the pre-eminence of the positive over the negative, for pleasure over pain, is the essence of the human drama.

The clash of the positive and the negative is illustrated in the world's greatest literature—the Greek tragedies, Shakespeare's plays, in the novels of Dickens, Dostoyevsky and Melville. Dante's The Divine Comedy portrays the "Inferno," a netherworld symbolic of the negative side. Dante's shadowy underworld is a place of suffering, and the allegory depicts an epic struggle between good and evil for the soul of man.

More recently, Luke Skywalker in the Star Wars series faces his inner demons who urge him to follow in the steps of his evil father Darth Vadar. "Come into the dark side of the force," the father begs his son. Luke must use all his inner resources to resist the seductive appeal of the dark side. Literature, myths, and legends tell us that true heroism is the adventure of self-discovery and the pursuit of liberation from an oppressive negative force.

Jill, in recovery from drug and alcohol abuse, revealed this human struggle when she said in a session, "I'm feeling a build-up of pressure. I'm being tempted to get back to drinking and drugging. You know what it is—I want to be bad. I can really feel how much I want to be bad. It's fun and exciting and hard to resist."

Jill had felt shamed, criticized, and disapproved of during her childhood, and through that experience she had acquired a secret unconscious attachment to those feelings. As an adult, she saw others as criticizing her and disapproving of her, and unconsciously she indulged in these negative feelings. In fact, her impulse to drink and to take drugs was caused in part by her conviction that she was a bad person. Consciously, however, she was only aware of her suffering—her fear of relapsing and the waves of self-reproach and self-condemnation that washed over her whenever she acted out with her addictive behavior. She gave herself the condemnation she was unconsciously looking for from others.

The dark side of our nature is symbolically represented as the dragon's liar in the legends of brave knights and beautiful damsels, in the tragic undercurrents of the Iliad and the Odyssey, in the tales of Siegfried and St. George. Ancient heroes and heroines liberated themselves from sinister villains and evil forces in their savage world. The archetypal image of a devil is based on the intuitive awareness of a sinister power entirely opposed to our well-being.

Where do secret attachments to negative emotions fit in this struggle between the negative and the positive? Meta-phorically, secret attachments to negative emotions are like black holes of outer space. Black holes cannot be seen directly and no light escapes from them because of their extreme gravity. In a comparable way, very little light shines on secret attachments because they are in the unconscious mind behind a heavy curtain of psychological defenses. Black holes are detected by their gravitational influence on other bodies or energy systems in their vicinity. Secret attachments are detected and understood through our patterns of self-defeat, our misery, substance abuse, compulsive behavior, obsessions, phobias, and by our negative impact on others.

The addictive personality is pulled into the negative vortex within himself. Like mass in a black hole, he becomes rigid, closed, contracting, trapped in an inner darkness that makes him feel powerless. The addictive personality is aware only of the outer manifestations of his secret attachments which include stress, dissatisfaction, boredom, worry, fear, guilt, anger, hurt, anxiety, confusion, loneliness, dissension, depression, shame, self-absorption, and so on. . .

Each child, because of the self-centeredness he is born with, comes into the world predisposed to misinterpret the actions and intentions of the parents. Each child is encumbered by the negative impact of his parents' weaknesses and the subjective manner in which he interprets the actions and attitudes of his parents toward himself. In other words, infants and children personalize their experiences with their parents and siblings, misinterpret them, and tend to perceive that parents and siblings are against them in some manner. Childhood perceptions and emotions linger on to create emotional difficulties later in life.

Our present emotional reactions are the result of an interaction between our parents' influence on our upbringing, as well as our own personal way of interpreting how we were treated. We know that many addictive personalities have had good conventional upbringings. Moreover, many adults who have been raised in dysfunctional families have no addictive problems and manage their lives successfully. I have heard the anguish of hundreds of parents who are at a loss to explain their children's convictions of unfair treatment when these parents have gone out of their way to be fair with each child.

Even when parents were controlling or abusive, continuing animosity toward them (which can be repressed and unconscious) indicates the adult son or daughter is holding them responsible for his or her problems. In other words, the child, and later on the adult, continues to choose to hold onto feelings of hurt and insult. He is willing to be affected and recreate the same familiar feelings long after parenting stops. For example, consider an alcoholic who says angrily, "I would not be an alcoholic if my father had not been an alcoholic!" Even if this statement were true, the son's blaming attitude makes him feel less responsible for his own negative attitudes and behavior, and more prone to continue his self-damaging behavior.

He will use blame as a defense in other areas of his life to avoid seeing and being responsible for his own self-damaging tendencies. He will hold grudges against significant others in his life for the same problems he had with his father—feeling let down, a burden, unloved, and neglected. If he blames his parents, he is compelled to see significant others as pseudo-parents (transference) who he feels are also against him in some way. As long as he holds grudges against his father, he holds onto his secret attachments to feeling disappointed and unloved, and he unconsciously remains determined to be the victim of his father.

This does not mean that, in order to be healthy, a son or daughter has to admire or love parents who may have been negligent or cruel. Cases of incest or physical abuse, for instance, can negate all claims on love. For the person's sake, however, continuing to hold the parents responsible for his present-day problems will not serve a healthy purpose. . .

To recognize our secret attachments is to come to an inner realization that is both humbling and frightening, for such recognition requires that we come face-to-face with an alien and self-defeating force within ourselves. As it turns out, the more we see into this side of ourselves, the more we gain in strength and self-control.

As a group, addictive personalities represent a cross-section of the population who are in a more critical showdown with this alien side of their human nature.

Freud believed in a self-destructive element in the psyche. He called it the death drive, and wrote that it constituted a force of self-aggression directed at the inner person from what he called the super-ego. Freud's final thoughts on the death drive were published posthumously in *An Outline of Psychoanalysis*. In this text, the role of the pleasure principle and the death drive were presented as the cornerstone of his understanding of mental health. However, his followers were loath to accept this view, and they declined to incorporate it into mainstream psychoanalysis. There were inferences that a decline in Freud's intellectual powers as he approached his death had contributed to this "alien" intrusion into his psychological framework. Very few psychologists and psychotherapists incorporate into their clinical practice the understanding of such an alien force at work undermining the conscious hopes and aspirations of their patients.

The death drive does not mean that people secretly want to kill themselves. Rather, it refers to self-aggression or self-hatred, and our tendency to put ourselves in situations that oppose our well-being. The death drive opposes our mental, emotional, and spiritual evolution. It is personified in the self-destructive addict who starves himself emotionally, who denies himself pleasure and joy, who endangers his health while being held back and poisoned by his own negative impressions and self-absorption. . .

Try this as an exercise. Go through your day and observe how often you find yourself worried or caught up in negative expectations about others and how they will respond to you. Watch how you personalize the behavior of others. Keep an eye on your critical inner voices that put you down and discount your abilities.

Taking emotional responsibility means understanding how you maintain your dissatisfactions about yourself and life. You need to see how attached you are to this negative perspective, which means seeing how tempted you are to indulge in negative feelings. This insight brings about a shift in your perspective, resulting in better feelings about life and about yourself.